Ohio Confidential

ential

*Stories of sex, scandal,
murder, and mayhem by*
JOHN BOERTLEIN

Published by Clerisy Press
Printed in the United States of America
Distributed by Publishers Group West
First edition, first printing

Clerisy Press
1700 Madison Road
Cincinnati, OH 45206
www.clerisypress.com

Library of Congress Cataloging-in-Publication Data
Boertlein, John, 1957-
  Ohio confidential : sex, scandal, murder, and mayhem
in the Buckeye State / by John Boertlein.
       p. cm.
  Includes bibliographical references and index.
  ISBN-13: 978-1-57860-299-5
  ISBN-10: 1-57860-299-8
1. Crime--Ohio--History--Case studies.
2. Scandals--Ohio--History--Case studies.
I. Title.

  HV6793.O3B64 2007
  364.109771--dc22

  2007036028

Edited by
JACK HEFFRON

Cover and interior designed by
STEPHEN SULLIVAN

Cover photos appear courtesy of Photofest (Charles Manson, Traci Lords, Jerry Springer)
and the U.S. Library of Congress (Warren Harding).

Photos in *Ohio Confidential* appear courtesy of:
Photofest: 22, 26-27, 30, 134, 144, 146-147, 158, 260, 263, 276-277
The Cleveland State University Library, Special Collections: 18, 40-41, 58, 62-63, 78-79,
       82-83, 91, 97, 122, 126, 128, 130-131, 180, 183, 192-193, 265, 268
Delhi, Ohio, Historical Society: 12, 17, 19
The United States Library of Congress: 44, 50, 89, 90-91, 125, 148, 152-153, 196, 200,
       204, 209
The President's Daughter, by Nan Britton: 54-55
The United States Federal Corrections: 84, 96, 141
The Cincinnati Police Department: 98, 104-105, 107, 116-117
The Ashville Citizen-Times: 155
Cincinnati Magazine/Ryan Kurtz: 162
Cincinnati Magazine/Kevin Miyazaki: 163
Richard Hunt Photography: 167
The Toledo Blade: 168, 173, 174, 176-177
Summit County Sheriff's Office: 212
National Governor's Association: 218
Ohio Department of Corrections: 220
Ohio Historical Society: 225
Adams County (Illinois) Sheriff's Office: 234
Milwaukee County Sheriff's Office: 252-253

For John Stewart Beatty Boertlein,
my son the graduate
and
Kyla Nicole Boertlein,
my daughter the Senior.

For Andy and Chandra Schanie,
aspiring entrepreneurs.
The future is yours, kids. Achieve!

And for
Mary "Viva Las Vegas" Carol,
Rock-A-Hula, Baby!

Acknowledgments

Many thanks to Jack Heffron, without whom this book would not have been possible. Thanks also to Steve Sullivan, who created the look of the book, from the cover to the page layout, and provided invaluable creative input throughout the process. Diane Tenaglia and Kara Pelicano helped find many of the photos, spending many hours in the search, and I'm grateful for their efforts. Howard Cohen and Richard Hunt head up sales and marketing at Clerisy Press, and I appreciate their support in finding an audience of interested readers. Thanks, too, to all the folks at the historical societies and photo archives who provided the images in the book, especially Vern Morrison of the Digital Production Unit of the Cleveland State University library. And a special thanks to Linda Vaccariello and all the people at *Cincinnati Magazine*, where the chapters on Larry Flynt and Donald Martin first appeared in different form.

Table of

CONTENTS

Introduction

THOSE OF US BORN AND RAISED IN OHIO, AND EVEN THOSE
who are relatively new to the area, take a lot of pride in our fair
state. Great cities, beautiful countrysides, quaint little towns,
excellent universities, plenty of friendly folks. What's not to
like? And Ohio has produced a lot of exceptional people
through the years, from war heroes to sports stars, presidents
to inventors, and leaders in business and industry, science, the
arts, you name it. Why, heck, the first human being to walk on
the moon was a Buckeye!

If, like me, you're interested in state history, you know that
many books have been written about these great Ohioans.

This isn't one them.

Ohio Confidential, as the subtitle makes clear, is about sex,
scandal, murder, and mayhem. It provides a down-and-dirty
historical overview, if you will, of some of our less-than-
upstanding citizens. And we've had quite a few of them.

I've gotta be kiddin', right? No, I'm not. Sure, we Ohioans
have the reputation of being a bit on the bland side. People
from other places see us as mild-mannered, conservative, even
a little dull. But as you'll read in these pages, we've had a lot of
excitement here too.

"In Ohio?"

That's what some friends of mine said when I mentioned
the idea for this book to them. "Why don't you write about a
state like California or New York or Florida? Someplace where
there's a lot of that kind of action. Nothing juicy ever happens
in Ohio."

With a heart bursting with pride in my state, I said, "Hey, listen. Ohio has just as many serial killers, crooked politicians, pornstars, illicit lovers, and thieves as any other state. From crimes of passion to cold-blooded murder to outright treason, Ohio has it all."

And with this book, I set out to prove it. I think it's high time we cast off our reputation as a boring, goody-two-shoes locale where life is blissfully bland. Let's stand up and expose our seamy underbelly. When it comes to shocking, greedy, criminal, crazy, or downright sinful behavior, we don't have to take a backseat to anybody.

From the banks of the Ohio River just outside Cincinnati at the tomb of William Henry Harrison to the Kingsbury Run area of Cleveland, where Eliot Ness tracked a "Mad Butcher" near the shores of Lake Erie, the Buckeye State has many stories to tell. These tales from the heartland may involve tragedy, temptation, or titillation; they may shock or fascinate or move you. But they definitely won't bore you.

Whether they changed the face of American justice like Dolly Mapp or provided fodder for the tabloids and nude models for *Playboy* magazine, as in the case of Wayne Hays and Elizabeth Ray, some colorful characters called Ohio home. Some, like Charles Manson and Traci Lords, headed for the West Coast to make a name for themselves. Axis Sally followed her professor/lover all the way to Nazi Germany to gain infamy. Others stayed right here in the Buckeye State to make their marks on history.

So read on, if you will, and enjoy the seedy, sexy, sumptuous sides of Ohio that some never see.

GEORGE
REMUS

King
of the
Bootleggers

1

Wet in Cincinnati

George Remus

THE JAZZ AGE OF THE ROARING TWENTIES gave author F. Scott Fitzgerald plenty of material for his novels. None more than the real-life Prohibition-era bootlegger George Remus from Cincinnati. After a chance meeting of the two men at the luxury Seelbach Hotel in the heart of bourbon country, Louisville, Kentucky, Fitzgerald became so impressed with Remus's rags-to-riches story and the opulent lifestyle he had lived since, he made Remus the model for the title character of his most famous work, *The Great Gatsby*. Truth be known, however, Remus's real life may have been more suited for book pages than that of Jay Gatsby.

George Remus was born in Germany in the late 1800s. He immigrated to the United States with his parents when he was four years old. The family settled in Chicago, where Remus eventually got a job in an uncle's pharmacy at the age of nineteen. With a good sense for business, Remus owned two pharmacies by the time he was twenty-one. But soon the young man grew tired of the relatively tame pharmacy business, deciding instead to try his hand at law practice. By the age of twenty-four, Remus was admitted to the Illinois State Bar.

As an attorney, Remus enjoyed criminal defense work and, like most lawyers, wasn't above using theatrics for effect. One story puts Remus as defense counsel in the trial of a man accused of murder in the poisoning death of his wife. During closing arguments, Remus presented the jury with a bottle purportedly containing the remnants of the poison his client had used on his now-departed wife. "There has been a lot of talk about poison in this case," Remus suggested, "but it is a lot of piffle. Look." With that the lawyer upended the bottle, swallowing the remainder of its contents. The jury watched in amazement expecting lawyer Remus to drop over dead. Remus nonchalantly continued arguing his case. What the jurors didn't know was the defense attorney, a former pharmacist, knew the poison's antidote, which he took shortly before court. The defendant was acquitted.

By 1920 the Volstead Act brought Prohibition to the United States. Although Remus never touched alcohol, he found himself defending the suppliers of the masses who did. He was rather frank about his observation of the "bootlegging" business: "I was impressed with the rapidity with which those men, without any brains at all, piled up fortunes in the liquor business. I saw a chance to make a clean-up."

Never one to miss a business opportunity, Remus used his legal instincts to study the Volstead Act. What he found were opportunities to exploit loopholes in the law by legally manufacturing and distributing alcoholic beverages, then merely putting the booze into the hands of thirsty citizens. According to Remus, "Prohibition was wrong. It was not accepted by the great majority of people and therefore bootlegging was not criminal."

"Medicinal whiskey," provided through government bonded outlets, was completely legal. Remus soon discovered that over 80 percent of "legal" whiskey was manufactured within 300 miles of Cincinnati, Ohio, making the "Queen City of the West" a natural center for a bootlegging empire.

Remus arrived in Cincinnati with his divorcée girlfriend Imogene Holmes in 1919. He settled in by marrying the former Mrs. Holmes and buying his first distillery. A year later, Remus owned another dozen perfectly legal liquor distilleries and distribution centers. The cash rolled in. He and Imogene bought an opulent mansion, complete with indoor swimming pool, on Cincinnati's west side, where they frequently threw elaborate Gatsby-esque parties. The whiskey business soared, and Remus, being the owner of legal manufacturing and distribution outlets for his booze, faced only the logistics of supplying the huge demand of the general public. These problems he overcame, however, using some inventive schemes like siphoning the real whiskey out and refilling the barrel with water and grain alcohol or actually hijacking his own trucks. Widespread bribery of public officials aided the corporate requirements of Remus's empire. By the end of 1921, George Remus was known as the "King of the Bootleggers," a pretty grand title considering he was in company with men like Al Capone, Dutch Schultz, and Meyer Lansky.

In April of 1922, George Remus's luck ran out. He was indicted on numerous charges of violating the Volstead Act and, despite more bribes to high government officials and constant legal maneuvers, by January 1924 he found himself

Imogene (Holmes) Remus

serving time at the federal penitentiary in Atlanta. Hard time wasn't all that bad for Remus as he "greased" the right officials to garner himself a private cell with maid service, special food, and a cushy job in the prison library. Not wanting to sit still for long, George sought to get consideration for early release by finding favor with a young federal agent named Franklin Dodge. Remus provided Dodge information on other bootleggers or criminals he knew about. He even wrote

Bootlegging in the Roaring 20s was a risky business but despite occasional run-ins with the law, it made many men, including George Remus, rich. (inset) The Remus mansion.

to his wife, Imogene, asking her to persuade Dodge to help her husband's cause. Dodge refused to intervene on George's behalf, but even after denying the request, he strangely continued to be seen in the company of Mrs. Remus.

A couple of days prior to his release from prison, Imogene stunned George by suing for divorce. Not only that, but shortly after his return to Cincinnati, he found his bootlegging business completely gone. He also had a new legal problem. His immigration into the United States had become an issue, and deportation to Germany loomed. Upon finding his mansion empty of furniture and his possessions gone, Remus became

Now, you decomposed mass

convinced he was the dupe in a love affair between his wife and Agent Dodge, the handsome unmarried agent who used Remus as an informant. He decided to take matters into his own hands.

About an hour before the couple was due in domestic relations court on October 6, 1927, Imogene and her daughter from her first marriage, Ruth, got into a cab and started toward Mrs. Remus's lawyer's office. As they traveled toward downtown, Imogene noticed they were being followed. "My God, there's George in that car!" she told the cab driver, ordering him to speed up. He did but George's driver kept pace, pursuing the cab into Cincinnati's Eden Park. The pursuit ended when George 's driver overtook the cab, forcing it to a stop off the side of the road.

George jumped out of the car and charged toward the cab. Imogene tried to flee but George grabbed her yelling, "Now, you decomposed mass of clay, I've got you!"

"Oh, Daddy, you know I love you. Daddy don't do it!" Imogene screamed as her husband pulled a pearl-handled revolver from his pocket and pressed the barrel against her stomach. A single shot rang out. Bleeding, Imogene staggered into traffic begging for help. George 's driver had panicked at the sight and drove off. George simply strolled away from the scene. Imogene made it to the hospital, where she soon expired.

Remus turned himself into police and declared the killing a matter of principle. "I never smoked, drank, or swore in my life," he told reporters. "I cannot stand for the sort of thing this man and Mrs. Remus have been carrying on for a long time."

of clay, I've got you!

Remus pleaded not guilty by reason of insanity, a condition he said was exacerbated by the fact that Imogene's adultery was carried out with the former Prohibition agent Franklin Dodge. The trial lasted a little over a month with the defense painting a portrait of Mrs. Remus as a two-timing gold digger who squandered the fortune her husband had entrusted to her. The strategy worked: Remus was found not guilty by reason of insanity and, although he spent time at the State Hospital for the Criminally Insane at Lima, he was a free man by June 28, 1928.

By then most of his fortune had been squandered. Remus remained something of a local folk hero until he suffered a stroke in 1950. He died in relative obscurity on January 20, 1952.

JOHN
DILLINGER

Terrorizes

the Buckeye

State

2

Johnnie's Summer Vacation in Lima

John Dillinger

THE BUCKEYE STATE OF THE 1930s SUFFERED through the Great Depression with the rest of the United States. Times were hard, and people were worried. Some say they needed a hero, a Robin Hood, perhaps, to deliver the common man from the wretches of foreclosing banks and the government establishment. Whatever the case, John Dillinger, despite being a violent ex-convict, found fame in a rip-tear crime spree across Ohio and the Midwest. North to south and in between, the "Dillinger Gang" murdered, robbed, and pillaged across Ohio in a rampage that made legends of the gang and brought to prominence what has become the preeminent law enforcement agency in the world, the Federal Bureau of Investigation.

Born in Indianapolis in 1903, John Dillinger's troubled youth led to an extended stint in Indiana's Pendleton penitentiary by the time he was twenty-two. There he met Harry Pierpont, who, like Dillinger, was handsome and soft-spoken, yet seemingly incorrigible when it came to the rather bad habit of robbing banks. After a failed escape attempt, Pierpont earned a transfer to Indiana's toughest penitentiary, in Michigan City. Dillinger also became friends with a petty thief named Homer Van Meter, who had a reputation for breaking prison rules while "clowning around." But what Van Meter saw as joking, the prison guards saw as the actions of a dangerous degenerate. He too was shipped off to Michigan City Penitentiary (MCP).

Dillinger's stay at Pendleton grew lonely for the young inmate, so after being denied parole in 1929, he stunned the parole board by requesting a transfer to Michigan City. He wanted to reunite with his friends, Pierpont and Van Meter, but he told the board he wanted the transfer because MCP had a better baseball team, and he wanted to play shortstop. The transfer was granted.

Back with his pals at Michigan City, Dillinger soon found himself accepted into an elite circle of company—bank robbers. By the time Dillinger arrived, Harry Pierpont had assembled an entourage of would-be pro bank job specialists. He enlisted the help of Herman "Baron" Lamm, a former Prussian army officer turned successful bank robber, to school the bank-robbing students. Lamm's first lesson was instructing his eager students to carefully study the layout of the target bank, locating the safes and finding out who could open them. Then came the rehearsal stage in which each gang member was given a specific job and an exact time in which to finish it. The gang was taught to leave the bank under a strict timeline—with or without the money. The

Pierpont pulled a gun and said, "Here's our credentials," and shot the lawman twice.

John Dillinger's gang has its day in court in 1933.
(left to right) Russell Clark, Charles Makely, Harry Pierpont,
John Dillinger, Ann Martin, Mary Kinder.

last step was determining and swiftly rehearsing an escape plan.

By now, Pierpont's class of bankrobbing included "Fat Charley" Makley, a forty-year-old veteran bank robber from Ohio; John "Red" Hamilton, an ill-tempered thirty-four-year-old veteran bank man; Russell Clark, a relative newcomer to the bank robbery business who was doing time after only one foiled attempt; and John Dillinger, Pierpont's up-and-coming protégé. Every individual in the group except Dillinger faced long prison terms. Dillinger, then, was the natural choice to be the outside man in the prison escape plan for the rest of the boys.

By May 1933, after four years at Michigan City, Dillinger managed to gain parole. A couple weeks after his release, he rounded up two friends of Pierpont's who agreed to help begin collecting money to finance a scheme to spring the MCP bunch. The group knocked off the New Carlisle National Bank in New Carlisle, Ohio, to the tune of an incredible ten thousand Depression-era dollars. Drugstore and supermarket robberies followed, but Dillinger found his cohorts "incompetent." When they were arrested, he simply went down Pierpont's list, finding more accessories to acquire the cash needed to pull off the gang's prison escape.

Johnnie D. made his way to Dayton, Ohio, where he hooked up with Mary Longnaker, a young divorcée. Her brother was serving time in Michigan City; he had told Dillinger of his "good-looking" sibling. It wasn't long before the Dayton police discovered the location of a boarding house where Dillinger had taken a room across from Mary's. Two detectives took a room in the same house and regularly read Mrs. Longnaker's mail to try to determine Dillinger's next visit. Before returning to Dayton, however, Dillinger managed to set the stage for the gang's elaborately planned escape from the penitentiary. Achieving his mission, he returned to the boarding house to await his group's arrival. He was arrested in no time. Pierpont and company were only days away from a daring prison break and "Johnnie Boy" was, ironically, on his way to the pen.

En route back to Michigan City, Dillinger was housed in the Allen County jail in Lima, Ohio. From there he wrote to his father: "Hope this letter finds you well and not worrying too much about me. Maybe I'll learn some day, Dad, that you can't win at this game. I know I have been a big disappointment to you but I guess I did too much time for where I went in a care-free boy and came out bitter toward everything in general. Of course, Dad, most of the blame lies with me, for my environment was of the best but if I had gotten off more leniently when I made my first mistake this never would have happened.... I am well and treated fine. From Johnnie."

In fact, Dillinger was being treated quite well by Sheriff Jess Sarber and his wife, who lived in the jail building and often took their meals with the prisoners. Meanwhile, Harry Pierpont and the other escapees headed toward Lima looking to free their captured comrade.

Soon after Pierpont and company blew into town, he and two henchmen, armed with pistols, went to the Lima jailhouse. Sheriff Sarber and his wife were finishing dinner in their office with a deputy. Pierpont told the sheriff he was an officer from Michigan City and wanted to see Dillinger. When Sarber asked to see credentials, Pierpont pulled a gun and said, "Here's our credentials," and shot the lawman twice. Sarber reached for a pistol he kept in the desk drawer, but another assailant, Charley Makley, pistol whipped him over the head with his gun, accidentally firing a wild shot in the process. Mrs. Sarber quickly threw the jail cell keys to Pierpont, who freed Dillinger. The assassins ran to their car. Sheriff Sarber, badly wounded, told his wife, "Mother, I believe I'm going to have to leave you." He died an hour and a half later. Chalk up John Dillinger's entry into the world of murder and crime to a small Ohio city.

CHARLES ARTHUR

"PRETTY BOY"

FLOYD

Visits

Ohio

3

Pretty Boy
Joins the Club

JOHN DILLINGER WASN'T THE ONLY BANK robber to achieve infamy during the early 1930s in Depression-ravaged America. Charles Arthur "Pretty Boy" Floyd pulled his share of jobs on Ohio banking institutions. Pretty Boy even met a bloody end in the Ohio countryside despite a self-made promise years before to avoid the state because of the bad luck he'd had there.

Charles Arthur Floyd, "Choc" to his friends, was born into a Georgia family in 1904. At an early age he migrated with his folks to Oklahoma, where they farmed in the rural Cookson Hills area. As a teen, Choc earned cash by picking cotton and it was here he fell in with "the wrong kind of people," who taught him there were easier, if not exactly legal, ways to earn a buck than enduring the backbreaking task of picking cotton. Charley Floyd showed signs of settling down for good when he married a local girl and moved into a house before the couple had their first child in 1924. But by summer of 1925, the new-lywed couldn't resist the temptations of easy cash promised by a friend he met in the cotton fields. John Hildebrand, a nine-teen-year-old thief who carried a gun and was reputedly on the run from the police, bragged to Floyd he had recently robbed a St. Louis company of $1,900 and there "was plenty more where that came from." Hildebrand assured Choc if the two were to team up, the scores would be big and much adventure would be had.

So Choc Floyd and John Hildebrand became partners in crime, pulling off robberies in a half-dozen food stores and gas stations for almost a month before they met up with a small-time hoodlum named Joe Hlavarty, a friend of Hildebrand's who knew of a pending payroll delivery at Kroger Food Store's main office in Kansas City. The three managed to hold up the payroll office for $11,500 in cash in what was described as a "quick, pro-fessional robbery." But the fellows proved their naiveté when they used some of the cash to buy a brand new Studebaker and showed it off on the streets of Ft. Smith, Arkansas. It didn't take long before the trio was arrested. Hildebrand confessed to the Kroger robbery, which had garnered national attention, includ-ing a report that the Kroger office manager had described one of the robbers as "a mere boy—a pretty boy with apple cheeks." Newspapers repeated the moniker "Pretty Boy" Floyd over and over. Charles Arthur Floyd had earned a new nickname, one he would hate but live with the rest of his life. He also got five years in a Missouri penitentiary.

Just like John Dillinger, Floyd found prison to be the Ivy League of schools for crime. And, like Dillinger, he chose bank robbery as his major. He found a willing and capable instructor in Kansas City bank robber Alfred "Red" Lovett, who promised to help his protégé get established in the world of bank robbery. And so when Floyd exited the Missouri State Penitentiary on March 7, 1929, he headed to Kansas City for an apprenticeship. By New Year's Day, 1930, Pretty Boy Floyd had joined the Jim Bradley Gang, which was heading to the areas around Toledo and Akron with plans to rob numerous banking establishments.

Bradley had met young Floyd in the prison yard at Missouri State. He was more than happy to add Floyd to his Ohio enterprise. Along with Floyd and Bradley, the gang included experienced bank robber Nathan King and nationally known shoplifter Nellie Maxwell.

The gang's first efforts in Ohio yielded slight rewards, the biggest take being $2,000 from the Farmer's & Merchant's Bank of Sylvania, Ohio, where an alert cashier managed to stash "twenty thousand in cash, negotiable Liberty Bonds, and jewelry" into a time-lock safe just as the thugs burst into the bank.

For three months the criminal quartet eluded authorities in the northern Ohio countryside. The uninterrupted spree ended on March 8, however, when two Akron police officers spotted them sitting curbside in a car in the middle of downtown. When the lawmen drew their vehicle alongside the gang's car, Bradley panicked and hit the gas, crashing into another automobile and throwing King out into the street. King surrendered immediately, but Bradley pulled a pistol and fired point-blank into Officer Harland F. Manes's abdomen killing him. Officer

Kovach returned fire, wounding the fleeing Bradley, who still managed to escape on foot into the crowded business district alone. He would later hook up with Floyd and Maxwell back at the hideout.

It is likely King told the police everything he knew. Hours after the murder, several dozen Akron-area detectives broke down the door of the gang's hideout and found Floyd and Maxwell tending to Bradley's wounds. King later described what the detectives found in the gang's preparation for a quick departure: "Bags were packed, a machine gun, with a clip of 150 bullets, was wrapped in a blanket where the gangsters were found. Three sets of license plates were found for Ohio, Indiana and Michigan. There was also a set of very expensive luggage, nitroglycerine and rubber gloves. Parked outside was a stolen car with glass removed from the back window to make room for a machine gun muzzle."

The subsequent trial brought a death sentence for Jim Bradley for the murder of Officer Manes. For their robbery spree throughout Ohio, Pretty Boy Floyd, Nellie Maxwell, and Nathan King each got fifteen years in the Ohio State Penitentiary. Rumor has it that when Jim Bradley was strapped into the electric chair, also known as "Ol' Sparky," in November of 1930, he told those present, "If you think I'm tough, boys, wait until you get a load of that Floyd." If they didn't believe Bradley's words that day, they soon would.

Under armed guard en route by train from Akron to the Ohio State Penitentiary in Columbus, Pretty Boy Floyd convinced the guards to take off his handcuffs while he used the bathroom. Granting him some privacy, the guard stood outside as Pretty Boy conducted his business. When the sentry heard breaking glass, he burst into the tiny compartment only to find a silhouette hightailing it into the sunset. By the time they could stop the train, the only sign of Charles Arthur Floyd was a dirty footprint on a pane of glass lying beside the tracks.

Floyd returned to Kansas City as a fugitive. That didn't stop him from getting another partner in William "Billy the Baby-Faced Killer" Miller and heading back to the Buckeye State. Accompanying the boys were sisters Rose and Juanita Baird. After staging holdups in Kentucky and Whitehouse, Ohio, the group headed toward Toledo. More trouble in Ohio ensued when Rose and Juanita wanted to do some shopping in downtown Toledo's Uhlman's Department Store. A clerk recognized Pretty Boy from a post office wanted poster and immediately phoned police. Officers arrived swiftly and waited for the quartet outside on a busy Toledo sidewalk. As the four exited Uhlman's, Toledo's top officer, Police Chief Galliher, ordered their surrender. Floyd and Miller responded with blazing pistols. The bandits tried to edge their way toward their auto, but Miller took a bullet in the chest and dropped dead on the pavement. A ricochet hit Juanita Baird in the back of the head, and she fell wounded. Rose cried out and threw herself upon her collapsed sister. Now alone in the fight, Pretty Boy continued to maneuver his way toward the gang's car. A police officer stepped out from cover to get a better view, giving Floyd the opportunity to pump several rounds into his stomach. The police chief returned fire, but his aim was poor. Floyd managed to reach his vehicle and made tracks out of Toledo. Ohio was nothing but trouble for him; he vowed never to return.

Floyd decided the only place he might be able to hide was the Crookson Hills he knew so well. Since his last visit to Oklahoma, the Great Depression had devastated the area. Wall Street had crashed, and the Great American Dust Bowl days of drought were just beginning. By destroying mortgages and promissory notes during his robberies, Pretty Boy used the unusual opportunity to become the "Robin Hood of Oklahoma" and the "Phantom of the Ozarks" to his ever-growing "common

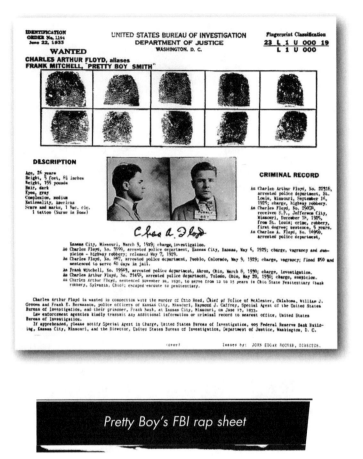

Pretty Boy's FBI rap sheet

folk" fan base. After suffering fifty-one stick-ups by Floyd in 1931 alone, bankers demanded that Oklahoma Governor "Alfalfa Bill" Murray call out the National Guard to apprehend Pretty Boy. Murray didn't see the need to waste the time or resources. "National Guard?" he replied. "As long as he stays down there where he's at and is protected the way he is by those people, he will continue to rob banks—National Guard or not!"

Charley enjoyed his legendary can't-be-touched persona as

"Pretty Boy" in the backwoods of Oklahoma until an incident occurred miles away from the hills in Kansas City that, some say unjustly, earned the hero-criminal a charge of cold-blooded murder. The "Kansas City Massacre" occurred on June 17, 1933. A group of federal agents and police officers were transporting a high-profile fugitive, Floyd's friend Frank Nash, when they were ambushed near a Kansas City train station. The law officers and the fugitive were all shot to death in a hail of machine gun and shotgun fire. Despite shoddy or weak evidence, J. Edgar Hoover, chief of the agency that would later become the Federal Bureau of Investigation, quickly implicated Pretty Boy Floyd and then-partner Adam Richetti in the crime largely because of his disdain for the elusive pair and the duo's association with Nash. The day

"If you think I'm tough, boys, wait

after the massacre, Hoover took to the radio waves telling the nation: "No time, money, or labor will be spared toward bringing about justice to the individual responsible for this cowardly, despicable act. They must be eliminated. And to this end we are dedicating ourselves."

Charley Floyd denied participation in the Kansas City Massacre until the end. Most evidence supports his claim. But it didn't matter at the time, and Floyd surmised he had to get out of the Oklahoma hill country he had always called home. Ironically the first place he went was Cleveland, Ohio, where he sought the help of local gangster Moe Dalitz. But even Dalitz's places became too hot with federal agents constantly asking questions about Pretty Boy. Charley had already had two rotten experiences in Ohio, and some say he was superstitious about tempting fate with a third. Floyd and partner

Richetti, accompanied again by Rose and Juanita Baird, decided to go to a place where Pretty Boy would be less known. They loaded the car and started for Buffalo, New York.

While Pretty Boy Floyd cooled his heels in Buffalo, things were changing for the feds. The Federal Fugitive Act gave the FBI the right to pursue anyone who had crossed state lines to avoid prosecution. Things in Buffalo were going okay for the gangsters, but Floyd soon became homesick and made several trips back to Oklahoma to visit family. He also took some time out to meet up with John Dillinger and company for a bank job in Indiana.

But three months after Dillinger's fatal ambush in Chicago at the hands of the FBI's up-and-coming super-agent Melvin Purvis, Chief Hoover announced all of Purvis's attention would

until you get a load of that Floyd."

be directed toward apprehension, dead or alive (though most believed more likely dead), of the nation's "most wanted public enemy": Charles Arthur "Pretty Boy" Floyd.

Charley figured he had only one option: escape to Mexico beyond Purvis's reach. First he wanted to go back to the hills to offer family the opportunity to join him. On Thursday, October 18, 1934, Pretty Boy, Richetti, and the Baird sisters got into their eight-cylinder Ford leaving Buffalo headed for the Cookson Hills.

By October 20, the group had made it as far Wellsville, Ohio. One can't help but wonder if Pretty Boy Floyd was uncomfortable with returning to Ohio, the place he always encountered "bad luck." Adam Richetti was driving in a dense fog on Interstate Route 7 between Wellsville and East Liverpool, Ohio, when he lost his bearings and struck a telephone pole.

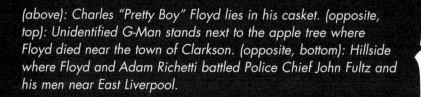

(above): Charles "Pretty Boy" Floyd lies in his casket. (opposite, top): Unidentified G-Man stands next to the apple tree where Floyd died near the town of Clarkson. (opposite, bottom): Hillside where Floyd and Adam Richetti battled Police Chief John Fultz and his men near East Liverpool.

Being cautious and perhaps justifiably paranoid, Charley told the girls to head back for help at a service station they had passed. When the car was repaired, the sisters could pick up the men and they would continue their trip. Rose and Juanita complied while Charley and Adam found a place to relax along the road at Elizabeth Hill.

The next morning, two locals were on their way into Wellsville when they noticed two men sitting near the tree line and wondered why two strangers in suits and ties would be camped in the grass a couple miles from town. In Wellsville they reported their suspicions to Police Chief John Fultz, who decided to investigate. The chief and two other men walked toward East Liverpool, where they found the pair sitting along Route 7. As the investigators approached, Richetti took off into the brush. Fultz's companions gave chase while the lawman faced the second stranger. Pretty Boy produced his automatic pistol and shot at the chief but missed. Fultz fired on Floyd, also missing. The ensuing gun battle ended when Fultz was struck in his foot. With the policeman shot, Pretty Boy managed to flee into the tree line and the forest behind.

Melvin Purvis was working another case in Cincinnati but immediately went to East Liverpool when he got the news. With Purvis were agents Hall, Hopton, and McKee. When Floyd was spotted in East Liverpool, Purvis organized a search party to which he added local volunteers—one of whom was World War I sharpshooter Chester Smith. "I have a feeling we're closing in," Agent Purvis told the party.

By Monday afternoon on October 22, 1934, Pretty Boy Floyd was tired and hungry. He stopped at an East Liverpool farmhouse where the Widow Conklin showed hospitality to the stranger with a hot meal and place to clean up. Floyd talked the widow's brother-in-law into a ride to Clarkson, where he figured he could rest and clearly plan a getaway. As he waited for the driver, he noticed two carloads of men cruising down Spruceville Road. He bolted for the woods.

"That's our boy," Purvis shouted as the heavily armed men gave chase. Pretty Boy approached the woods when Chester Smith took aim and fired, winging the fugitive in his right arm. The shot knocked him down, but soon he was back up and on the run. A second shot rang out, striking Pretty Boy in the back. This time he did not get up.

The official account has Purvis confirming Floyd's identity as he lay dying in that Ohio field. But the coroner's report noted that Pretty Boy Floyd's body had *three* bullet holes. It wasn't until 1979 that Chester Smith finally cleared up the mystery by revealing to *Time* magazine that Pretty Boy had been sprawled wounded in the field when Purvis questioned him about the Kansas City murders. When Floyd continued to deny any part in the massacre, Purvis ordered another agent to execute the fugitive, and the subordinate complied.

PRESIDENT
WARREN G.
HARDING

Loves the
Ladies

4

The Ladies' Man from Marion Goes to Washington

President Warren G. Harding

OHIO HAS SPAWNED MORE THAN ITS SHARE OF controversial politicians, perhaps none more than the twenty-ninth president of the United States, Warren G. Harding. Born in 1865 in Blooming Grove, Ohio, to prominent country physician George Harding and schoolteacher Phoebe Dickerson Harding, young Warren grew up in the small nearby town of Marion, the eldest of eight children. A graduate of Ohio Central College, Harding found his first real job as editor of the *Marion Times Star* newspaper, a daily he co-owned with his father, who maintained his medical practice across the hall in the same building in downtown Marion.

Young Harding was handsome and charming. He prospered on the local scene and found himself popular with the ladies. He caught the eye of divorcée Florence "Flossie" DeWolfe, an heiress-apparent of the wealthiest family in town who was five years older than Harding and with a son by her common-law husband. They married in 1891 over the staunch objections of Florence's father, Amos Kling, a business rival of Harding's who, according to biographer John Dean, tried to defame his son-in-law by claiming Harding's ancestry was African-American. (This rumor would surface throughout Harding's political career despite proof to the contrary.)

The Marion Republican found his way into politics in 1895 when he ran for, and lost, a bid for auditor of traditionally Democratic Marion County.

Not one to be denied, Harding again ran for political office with the help of the shrewd and savvy Flossie, whom he had dubbed the "Duchess" because of her arrogant demeanor and quick temper, which she apparently inherited from her father. This time Harding managed to be elected to a senate seat in the Ohio General Assembly in 1899. A stint as lieutenant governor followed in 1904 and 1905 when Harding took a break from politics to tend to his wife's failing health. But Warren became restless in private life. Between 1905 and 1910 Amos Kling and Harding had reconciled any differences and Florence's health improved. Harding made a bid for the Ohio governor's mansion in 1910, and lost. He seemed to lose interest in politics until 1914. Kling had died the year before, leaving the Hardings financially comfortable, with the idea of a Washington, D.C. residence appealing to both. The couple became Senator and Mrs. Warren G. Harding.

By 1920, Harding's political star had risen. He was elected by popular vote to the highest office in the land, the presidency of the United States of America. Thus began the presidential legacy of the man from Marion.

In a little more than three years as president, he was accused of a number of improprieties, most famously the "Teapot Dome scandal," which involved Harding's secretary of the interior, Albert Fall, who sold access to oil on federal land. This scandal was eclipsed by Harding's series of sexual indiscretions with a pair of fellow Ohioans from his beloved hometown of Marion.

Carrie Phillips, nine years younger than Harding, was a pretty strawberry-blond schoolteacher and the wife of Marion department store owner and longtime Harding friend Jim Phillips. In 1904, tragedy struck the Phillips household when the couple's four-year-old son, Jim Jr., suddenly died. Mr. Phillips became quite distraught. At the suggestion of his friend Harding, Jim decided to take a sabbatical at a Michigan sanatorium where Warren had spent time years before while suffering from nervous exhaustion.

> The Seventh Anniversary
> I love you more than all the world
> Possession wholly imploring
> Mid passion I am oftime whirled
> Oftimes admire—adoring
> Oh God! If only fate would give
> Us privilege to love and live!
> —*Warren G. Harding to his lover Carrie Phillips*
> *in a letter dated Christmas, 1915, which, oddly, would*
> *mean it had been eleven years since the affair began*

During the mister's absence, Warren called on Mrs. Phillips, presumably to console her. Warren found Carrie alone in her bedroom, where the "comfort" he offered became sexual. Harding found the "love of his life" that day and began an affair that lasted on and off for fifteen years.

With their spouses apparently oblivious, Warren and Carrie seemed to take every opportunity for adulterous playtime. When they were apart, they corresponded by mail that certainly qualifies as "lust letters" as much as "love letters."

"I love you garbed, but naked more," Harding wrote to his sweet mistress. In another letter, published in a 1976 edition of the *Washington Post*, he cooed, "There is one engulfing, enthralling rule of love, the song of your whole being which is a bit sweeter—Oh Warren! Oh Warren—when your body quivers with divine paroxysms and your soul hovers for flight with mine." Harding even tried his hand at poetry: "Carrie, take me panting to your heaving breast."

Although Warren seemed quite satisfied with the arrangement, Carrie occasionally demanded Mr. Harding leave his wife to marry her. In mortal fear of "the Duchess," and of ruining his political career, Warren steadfastly refused. By 1914, ten years into the affair, Florence Harding finally figured out what was going on and threatened Warren with divorce. He was able to talk her out of it though, while still managing to continue the affair for six more years. Jim Phillips didn't find out about his wife's infidelity until 1920, and probably not until Carrie told him. Although Carrie promised Warren she was destroying the love letters he wrote through the years, by 1920 and the presidential election, she became embittered at the Republican candidate and threatened to expose their adultery to the press by providing the sordid pages, which she had kept.

Candidate Harding responded by buying her a new Cadillac and offering $5,000 a year "in order to avoid disgrace in the public eye, to escape ruin in the eyes of those who have trusted me in public life."

When his offer appeared to fall short of her requirements,

Florence Harding

a nervous Republican National Committee got involved. They sent an emissary to Jim and Carrie Phillips, eventually getting them to agree to a payment of $20,000 and a trip around the world with an extended stay in the "Orient," plus $2,000 per month as long as Harding remained in office. Jim and Carrie graciously accepted the offer.

Like many others, they lost their financial security during the Great Depression. Jim Phillips succumbed to the bottle and died broke in 1939. Carrie developed a reputation as an eccentric until senility forced her into a nursing home, where she died in 1960. An attorney found Warren's love letters in her estate in 1963. According to Wesley Hagood, author of *Presidential Sex*, the letters are now in the possession of the Library of Congress and remain sealed under court order until July 29, 2014.

Amazingly, Warren Harding's extended affair with Carrie Phillips wasn't his only indiscretion, nor was it the most notorious. For several overlapping years and well into his presidency, Warren kept company with a young woman thirty-one years his junior—another Marion resident named Nan Britton. Nan was born in 1896 to a local physician and his school teacher wife who lived in the same neighborhood as the Hardings. By the time she was fourteen, Nan was already infatuated with Mr. Harding after seeing his picture on a Republican campaign poster in Marion. She apparently proclaimed her affection for Harding to anyone willing to listen.

The crush remained innocent enough until 1917, when Nan wrote to the Ohio senator upon her graduation from secretarial school inquiring about a letter of reference. More than happy to oblige, Senator Harding arranged a meeting with his young admirer to discuss her future. In May of that year, the two met in a reception room at the Manhattan Hotel in New York City. Small talk soon turned into discussion of Nan's early declarations of affection for Mr. Harding. It wasn't long before Nan confided to the senator that she still held those same feelings. Seemingly not surprised by the revelation, Warren suggested the two go up to his room where they could continue the discussion "without interruptions or annoyances."

"We had scarcely closed the door behind us when we shared our first kiss, it seemed sweetly appropriate," Britton later wrote, "I shall never forget how Mr. Harding kept saying, after each kiss, 'God!...God Nan!' in high diminuendo, nor how he pleaded in tense voice, 'Oh, dearie, tell me it isn't hateful to you to have me kiss you!' And as I kissed him back I thought that he surpassed even my gladdest dreams of him."

Although Nan claims their first encounter didn't go beyond the kiss, by July of 1917, she and Warren enjoyed regular sexual intimacies. Nan was rather naïve when it came to such matters, and so it was in 1919 on a trip to Senator Harding's Washington, D.C. office where the two made love that Britton says Harding's only child was conceived. In July of 1919, Elizabeth Ann was born. Mother and baby, albeit separately, attended the Republican National Convention the following August to watch Warren G. Harding win the Republican nomination for the office of president of the United States. They would not see each other again until after the election.

In her book *The President's Daughter*, Nan wrote of her first visit to President Harding in June of 1921:

> Whereupon he introduced me to the one place where, he said, he thought we might share kisses in safety. This was a small closet in the anteroom, evidently a place for hats and coats, but entirely empty most of the times we used it, for we repaired there many times during the course of my visits to the White House, and in the darkness of a space not more than five feet square, the President of the United States and his adoring sweetheart made love.

On at least one occasion Nan and President Harding were having sex in the White House closet when the Duchess, apparently tipped off by a Secret Service agent, tried to catch the two in the act. The president's bodyguard blocked the door, however, forcing the enraged Mrs. Harding to circle the mansion and enter through another door. By the time she got there, the president's man had managed to get Nan out a back door and all Florence found was a flustered Warren sitting sheepishly at his desk.

By January 1923 the president worried about the effects a scandal involving a mistress and illegitimate child would have on reelection. He told Nan his fears and added, according to Britton, that he would provide for mother and child as long as they lived. It was the last time they met. Harding died later that year, with no provisions left for Nan Britton or her daughter. Britton published *The President's Daughter* in 1927 and tells her story and the story of the "love child" she shared with Warren Harding. Although she was destitute by then and probably needed the money, Britton explained her motivation for writing the book as "the need for legal and social recognition and protection of all children in these United States born out of wedlock."

President Warren Harding died only 882 days into his only term in office, on August 2, 1923. His legacy of scandal, however, lives on despite biographer John W. Dean's book about Harding's life, which asserts: "While in office, Harding had his critics, as do all presidents, but few presidents have experienced the unrequited attacks and reprisals visited on one of the most kindly men ever to occupy the Oval Office. It hasn't been pretty." Dean describes his work as "not to challenge or catalogue those who have gotten it wrong about Harding, only to get it right."[1]

Right or wrong, President Harding's death precluded him from defending himself against any allegation. Even the cir-

---

[1] Dean is no stranger himself to presidential scandal. He's a convicted conspirator in the Nixon White House's Watergate investigation.

(above) A snapshot of Mr. Harding sent to Nan in June 1917;
(opposite, top) an account of the attempt to suppress the printing of
The President's Daughter; (opposite, inset) Nan with Elizabeth Ann
in 1921; (opposite, right) Nan Britton

SIX BURLY MEN

(and Mr. Sumner)

❧The *First Edition* of THE PRESIDENT'S DAUGHTER was hindered and trodden upon by interests which did not want to see this mother's true story given to the world. ❧On June 10, 1927, six burly New York policemen and John S. Sumner, agent for the Society for the Suppression of Vice, armed with a "Warrant of Search and Seizure," entered the printing plant where the making of the book was in process. ❧They seized and carried off the plates and printed sheets. ❧On June 29th, in a magistrate's court, the case was dismissed. The seized plates and printed sheets were returned to the publishers — the ELIZABETH ANN GUILD, Inc. - 20 West 46th St., New York.

cumstances of the president's demise became fodder for scandal. By the time he was laid to rest at the Warren Harding Memorial in his hometown of Marion, there were theories and speculation about what sent President Harding to the grave.

By today's standards, Warren Harding's lifestyle made him the perfect candidate for a heart attack. He lived the "high life" in pre-Prohibition America with a fat-filled diet complemented by regular tobacco and alcohol consumption. Exercise for the president consisted mostly of rounds of golf and twice-weekly poker games, accompanied by the occasional off-the-cuff love trysts. Natural causes seemed a perfectly plausible explanation. But one of Harding's attending doctors in San Francisco that August was Dr. Joel Boone, who (according to his diaries

"I love you garbed,

and memoirs as mentioned in the online Crime Library, www.crimelibrary.com) felt a physician's negligence may have contributed to Harding's demise. According to Boone, Harding's primary physician, Dr. Charles Sawyer, attributed the president's symptoms of angina to indigestion compounded by ptomaine poisoning from "a mess of king crabs drenched in butter." Sawyer administered "powerful purgatives" to Harding that eventually sent the patient into cardiac arrest. Of four physicians present, only Sawyer seemed to believe that stroke, the official cause of death was accurate. The other three, particularly Boone, believed it was heart attack, prompted by Dr. Sawyer's powerful purgatives, which killed the president. According to Crime Library, the other three physicians most likely agreed with Sawyer's diagnosis to protect his reputation from being damaged for malpractice involving the president of the United States.

Doctor's malpractice is only one of four scandalous theories surrounding Warren Harding's unexpected death. Others surmised the president committed suicide because of the political damage from the Teapot Dome scandal. Crime Library takes the suicide theory a couple steps further, exploring the possibility President Harding was murdered: for political reasons by those involved, or exposure of involvement in Teapot Dome; or the unlikely speculation that the Duchess did it with the dual motives of protecting Warren's reputation and as a form of revenge for her husband's adulterous ways.

Has history been unfair in its treatment of Warren Harding? Is a president's sex life a private matter not to be

but naked more."

scrutinized by the public? Perhaps the answers lie in Dean's conclusion to *Warren G. Harding* in which he quotes a poem read by Harding's secretary of state, Charles Evans Hughes, at a memorial eulogy delivered to the joint session of Congress on February 28, 1924:

> *Let who has felt compute the strain*
> *Of struggle with abuses strong,*
> *The doubtful course, the helpless pain*
> *Of seeing best intents go wrong.*
> *We, who look on with critic eyes,*
> *Exempt from actions crucial test,*
> *Human ourselves, at least are wise*
> *In honoring one who did his best.*

ELIOT
NESS

and the
Cleveland
Torso
Murders

5

The Untouchable Stalks
the Mad Butcher

Eliot Ness

LIKE MOST OF AMERICA, THE 1930s FOUND Cleveland's Kingsbury Run area struggling with the effects of the nation's Great Depression. But another, more purposeful evil added to the area's misery: a string of gruesome murders lasting three long years, taking its toll on an already stressed police department, and dethroning an American law enforcement icon along the way.

In the early-morning hours of September 5, 1934, a young man searching the water's edge for firewood found what appeared to be a tree stump on the banks of Lake Erie. Taking a closer look, Frank LaGassie discovered the first of a string of butchered murder victims in what would become Ohio's, and indeed one of the nation's, most gruesome and ultimately unsolved serial murder cases.

What LaGassie thought was driftwood was actually the lower torso of a woman, legs cut off at the knees, who had been in the water for an estimated three or four months. County coroner Arthur Pearce noted the carcass had been treated with some kind of substance, giving it a reddish appearance and probably preserving it in some way.

After reading an account of the find in a local newspaper, a man named Joseph Hejduk contacted the county sheriff's office about something he came across two weeks earlier on the shores of Lake Erie in North Perry, thirty miles to the east of Cleveland. Hejduk had found what appeared to be the vertebrae and rib cage of a human body with scraps of rotting flesh still attached. When Hejduk showed his find to Special Deputy Melvin Keener at the time, the deputy judged them to be animal bones and had Hejduk bury them on the sandy beach.

Subsequent comparison of what were now identified as body parts showed they were pieces of the same corpse. Unable to identify the remains and unaware of what the future held, the investigation of the woman dubbed in the press as "The Lady of the Lake" received only cursory attention, and the case was systematically filed.

Cleveland's Kingsbury Run area is a wide gorge covering the southeast portion of the city's industrial area in the Flats out to East 90th Street. It is bordered on the north by Woodland Avenue and on the south by Broadway. Originally named for one of the area's first settlers, James Kingsbury, it was a favorite picnic spot

The Kingsbury Run area during the time of the murders.

for residents in the late eighteenth and early nineteenth centuries because of its parklike setting. By the time of the Great Depression, however, Kingsbury Run had deteriorated into an industrial wasteland with row upon row of railroad tracks, a deep, polluted channel of water, and hobo camps set up among the weeds and debris.

It was here on September 23, 1934, that two boys tossing softball on Jackass Hill, one of the slopes leading down to the Run on its south side, near East 49th and East 50th Streets, made a startling discovery and sparked the legend of "The Mad Butcher of Kingsbury Run."

Going down the hill to retrieve their ball, the boys discovered a nude, headless, decomposing body lying on its side. The Erie Railroad police, charged with security at the train yards, were called to the site. There they found the body of a white male, nude with the exception of black socks, emasculated and decapitated, lying in the heavy brush. The absence of any blood in the area was an early indication the murderer committed the crime elsewhere and dumped the evidence of his crime down Jackass Hill. About twenty feet away, the head of the victim was found buried with a small amount of hair sticking out above the surface, apparently to ensure discovery.

By the time the Cleveland police arrived, their railroad counterparts had found the body of a second victim about thirty feet away. Although this body, also a white male, was shorter, older, and stockier than the first, its condition was similar, having the head and genitalia cut off.

Cleveland police officers began a thorough search of the area and found the head of the second victim about seventy feet from the body. The severed genitals of both victims were found together next to one of the bodies.

Clothing, some of which appeared blood soaked, was also found strewn about. The presence of blood on the clothing led the police to believe at least one of the men was dressed during the killing, then stripped and his body washed clean. County Coroner A.J. Pearce soon arrived and, although obvious and seemingly absurd, performed his official duty by declaring the men legally dead.

Dr. Pearce reported the autopsy results of both victims as, "Homicide by person or persons at present unknown. Death by decapitation, hemorrhage and shock." Decapitation was, and remains, a very unusual way of killing someone. One of the victims showed evidence of rope burns on both wrists, creating the horrible image of a man suffering almost surgical removal of his genitalia, neck, and head while fully conscious yet helpless with hands tied behind his back.

Police had little to go on. One of the men, the younger of the two, was eventually identified through fingerprints as Edward Andrassy, age twenty-eight. The Cleveland police were familiar with Andrassy as a small-time criminal with a taste for whiskey who was rumored to be bisexual. He had done time in the Warrensville Workhouse after a concealed weapons conviction and been arrested numerous times on intoxication charges. His family, Hungarian immigrants from a respectable background, were unable to provide any valuable leads to the police.

Andrassy's companion in death at the bottom of Jackass Hill was never identified. Investigators had little to go on other than theory. They speculated the unidentified victim's body, having been the first, was immersed in some sort of chemical liquid until Andrassy was done in and the two corpses could be disposed of together. They also believed each victim, hands bound behind him, was murdered by a sharp, heavy instrument, much like a butcher knife. Police also speculated the murderer, if there was only one, was a large, strong individual capable of carrying the bodies to the remote area at the bottom of Jackass Hill, which was inaccessible to automobiles or trucks. Despite the media attention created by the gruesome details of the murders, the police were at a standstill in bringing the perpetrator to justice.

Edward Andrassy and the unidentified man found butchered at the bottom of Kingsbury Run's Jackass Hill that September day in 1934 were to become known only as "Victim 1" and "Victim 2." As for "The Lady of the Lake," her identity remains a mystery. Although she was never officially described as a victim of the Mad Butcher of Kingsbury Run, the evidence earned her a place in history as "Victim 0." The murders soon found their way into the obscurity of "old news."

By November of 1935, Cleveland was tiring of the hangover left by mobsters, bootleggers, and the ensuing political and law enforcement corruption created by Prohibition. Republican Harold Burton was elected the city's mayor on the pledge to clean up crime and restore integrity to the police department. During the first month after taking office, Mayor Burton made good on his promise. He appointed Eliot Ness, the federal agent known as "untouchable" for bringing down Al Capone and the Chicago mob, as Cleveland's safety director to take control of the police and fire departments.

Ness wasted no time. He immediately implemented new strategies for hiring and training better-qualified police recruits, took the offensive against police corruption, and began an attack on gambling operations in the city. Shortly after taking over, he was introduced to the "Mad Butcher" through the discovery of the next victim.

January 26, 1936, found the city in the grip of bitter cold and snow, the type of weather that keeps most people indoors and keeps the streets calm and quiet. The residents of an apartment at 2340 East 22nd Street, however, found little peace. Dogs, left to the night, disturbed the silence of dawn with long, incessant howls. One of the residents grew weary of the noise and braved going outside to investigate. She found two baskets containing frozen meat. The woman apparently thought the baskets came from the White Front Meat Market at 2002 Central Avenue, so she went there to tell the market's owner, Charles Page, she had found "hams" down the alley behind his store. Page, believing he was the victim of a burglary, ran down the alley to make a stomach-turning discovery. The "hams" in actuality were dismembered pieces of a human body, left to freeze in the bitter cold.

The police were called, and the body parts—the lower half of a woman's torso, both of her thighs, and her right upper extremity—were taken to the coroner's office. Because the victim's right hand was present, fingerprints were available and police were able to identify Victim No. 3 as forty-two-year-old Florence Saudy Polillo, a heavy-drinking barmaid and sometime prostitute. Little else was determined about Flo Polillo's death until February 7, 1936, when her upper torso and thorax turned up in a yard behind a vacant house. The cold weather preserved the remains well enough for the coroner to determine the muscles in the victim's neck were retracted, meaning the cause of Flo Polillo's death was the cutting off of her head while she was still alive.

Like the three butchered bodies before hers, Flo Polillo's murder soon found its way to the police inactive investigations file. With no clues or leads to work with, the police had little choice. To date, no one had officially tied the four murders to a single suspect.

As far as Mayor Burton was concerned, Eliot Ness was doing a stellar job cleaning up Cleveland's image by reforming the police department and systematically striking at organized crime. Burton was quite proud to showcase his city in June 1936 when the Republican National Convention came to town. Ness knew his reputation and future rode on the success of security at the convention. He put in long hours personally overseeing every detail. If there was an impression of the city Ness wanted the visiting conventioneers to take back to America, it was of a modern, thriving downtown area, not of Kingsbury Run's dilapidated hobo camps, horribly polluted waterways, or soot-covered, and garbage-strewn wastelands.

His wish, however, was denied on the Friday before the convention was scheduled to begin. Two boys on their way to a fishing spot took a route through Kingsbury Run where they noticed a pair of rolled-up pants lying beneath a bush. When one of the boys curiously prodded at the clothing with his fishing pole, the decapitated head of a young man rolled out.

Terrified, the boys ran home where they waited until one of their parents arrived. The mother of one of the pair phoned police, who went to the scene in the late afternoon and located the gruesome discovery. The police initiated a search of the area for the rest of the body. The next morning they found the naked, headless corpse just east of the East 55th Street Bridge, about a thousand feet from where the boys stumbled upon the head and about eight hundred feet from the bottom of Jackass Hill, where the butchered bodies of Edward Andrassy and the other victim were found. The body was relatively fresh, and fingerprints could easily be taken. Also, the corpse bore various identifiable tattoos. Identification seemed imminent.

When the body was examined by the coroner, he determined the victim to be a white male in his early to mid twenties, five feet eleven inches tall and weighing about 165 pounds. Unlike Edward Andrassy and Victim No. 2, his genitalia were intact. The coroner described the cause of death as "decapitation and resulting shock." Despite fingerprints, several tattoos on the body, and clues offered by clothing found at the scene, the victim could not be identified. Police speculated he was merely a transient riding the rails who had unwittingly made the mistake of stopping at Kingsbury Run. Others opined he was too well-dressed and clean-shaven to fit the hobo profile. No blood was found in the area of the body's discovery. The fact that the body had been drained of blood and washed clean, an impossible task in Kingsbury Run, suggested the killing occurred elsewhere and the body moved to where it was discovered.

The coroner noted that killing an individual by decapitation was a very difficult thing to do. He also suggested a pattern was emerging—linking this death to Flo Polillo, the two men found in Kingsbury Run in 1935, and even "The Lady of the Lake." Perhaps because authorities were cognizant of the crime in their specific venue where "less equals better," the police chose to ignore the theory.

By the week of the convention, the story of a maniac killer on the loose was front-page news in every paper in the country. This was publicity Eliot Ness didn't want. Although Ness was convinced there was a single perpetrator, he gave explicit instructions to investigators not to suggest the thought in any way to the press. Concerned that conventioneers would be afraid to leave their hotel rooms if they thought there was a killer at large in the city, he ordered that absolutely no further information was to be released on the subject until the convention was over.

The convention went off without a hitch. Afterward, the city hosted the Great Lakes Exposition, a combination of amusement park entertainment and a World's Fair. The security of both events paid tribute to Safety Director Ness's planning and hard work. Homicide detectives continued to work on the case of the "tattooed man" but had found no promising leads or clues when they received a report that a teenage girl had discovered another headless corpse in the Big Creek area west of Cleveland.

Detectives found a dead man lying naked on his stomach. His head was approximately fifteen feet north of the body and partially wrapped in some clothing. Large amounts of dried blood suggested the victim was murdered at the site. The coroner speculated the body had been in the spot for two months or more, noting "the body was in an advanced state of decomposition with skin and flesh denuded in large areas. Rodents, maggots and the process of decomposition had removed portions of the internal viscera. The head had been separated from the body at the junction of the second and third cervical vertebrae, the ends of which bones showed no evidence of fracture." The coroner's determination that Victim No. 5 had been dead for "around two months" meant he was murdered at approximately the same time as Victim No. 4, the "tattooed man."

Decapitation had become the signature of the Mad Butcher. Ness concluded, as did the detectives working the case, that the

"Homicide by person or persons at present unknown.

murders were the work of a single killer. Although the newspapers published several sensationalized articles about the murders, the deaths of little-known or unknown lowlifes, prostitutes, or hobos took second page to high-profile gambling raids, crooked cops being busted, and a rapidly deteriorating mob hierarchy that reportedly considered shutting down operations in Cleveland as long as Eliot Ness was in town. A vicious serial killer was on the loose in Cleveland, but with little evidence other than the bodies and no real leads to go on, the police remained in a stalemate.

On September 10, 1936, a hobo sitting in the rail yard near East 37th Street in Kingsbury Run noticed something unusual floating in a stagnant, scum-filled puddle of the polluted creek running through the area. The vagrant recognized the refuse as pieces of a human body.

Detective Orley May reported: "We learned that the torso was discovered by Jerry Harris of St. Louis who was sitting on the pier alongside the creek, who noticed the two pieces of torso, who then notified the police. The torso was then removed from the creek and was sent to the county morgue. A search was immediately begun alongside the creek and the weeds for the balance of the body. The fire rescue squad was then called and the creek was dragged with grappling hooks with a view of recovering the remainder of the body in the outlet of this creek which comes out of a tunnel at this point, at which point the body was dumped over and small portions of flesh were found on a ledge where the torso struck when it was thrown over the ledge into the creek. We were unable to recover any portions of the body with the grappling hooks so we

Death by decapitation, hemorrhage and shock."

proceeded in using ceiling hooks and we recovered two legs below the knee. We then continued to search further and recovered the right thigh." A blood-stained shirt was also found wrapped in newspaper on the creek bank near where the body pieces were thrown in.

Hundreds of spectators watched from the perimeter as the detectives performed their morbid duty. Comments of shock and disgust swept through the crowd. By the time the local newspapers hit the stands, there was a name for the sick killer: "The Mad Butcher of Kingsbury Run." Word was out and Cleveland residents expressed a growing hysteria about the Mad Butcher who walked among them.

The coroner's report was all too familiar. He estimated the victim was a white male between twenty-five and thirty years old, approximately five feet ten inches tall and weighing around 145 pounds. The head had been surgically removed with two powerful cuts from the front and the back between the third and fourth cervical vertebrae. The torso was equally bisected, apparently by someone familiar with human anatomy. As with Edward Andrassy and Victim No. 2, the man had been emasculated. There were no signs of hesitation marks near any of the cuts. The coroner's report ruled "probable murder by decapitation and section of body." The *Cleveland News* quoted a deputy coroner as stating an examination of the victim's heart revealed he had been alive when the murderer began to dismember his body.

Victim No. 6's identity would likely remain a mystery without the recovery of his hands and head, so the police went to great lengths to search the creek and surrounding areas. Dragging hooks recovered the left thigh on September 12, but nothing else was found despite the efforts of a large contingent of the police force. During the search for the missing body parts, the Cleveland press reported thousands of curious onlookers and motorists went to Kingsbury Run to see for themselves. In the wake of the stalled investigation and ever-growing public alarm and publicity, Eliot Ness "officially" took over the investigation of the Mad Butcher of Kingsbury Run.

Despite his reputation as a super investigator, Ness was working with only the tools available to law enforcement in the 1930s. What he did know was a psychopathic maniac was at work. He allocated resources unprecedented in the history of the Cleveland police. He conferred with every officer involved in the case and sought the assistance of the county coroner. One of the detectives, Peter Merylo, eventually garnered full-time assignment to the case, often using unorthodox methods to track the butcher, such as going undercover dressed as a hobo and hanging around the Kingsbury Run area. But his efforts proved fruitless. A lot of work was being done but results were lacking, terribly lacking.

The saga continued when on February 23, 1937, history repeated itself and the bisected torso of a woman washed up on the Lake Erie beach at 156th Street, almost the same spot where pieces of the "Lady of the Lake" were found nearly three years earlier. This time the headless victim was deemed to be a woman, between the ages of twenty-five and thirty-five years. She weighed between 100 and 120 pounds and had been judged dead for approximately two or three days. Different from most of the other victims, blood clots in the woman's heart suggested she was decapitated after death. She became known simply as Victim No. 7; her arms, legs, and head were never found, and her identity remains a mystery.

Safety Director Ness's attempt to put a lid on newspaper reports of the Mad Butcher's activity, on the advice of forensic psychiatrists who believed the publicity fueled the killer's ego, became entangled with the political egos of others, including newly elected County Coroner Samuel Gerber. Gerber seemed to enjoy seeing accounts of his reports in the press, and Ness's suppression of the accounts caused a rift between the two. A lull in the feud between the two offices ended on June 6, 1937, when a young man located a rotting burlap bag with human remains under the Lorain-Carnegie Bridge four hundred feet west of Stone's Levee on the Cuyahoga River.

Dr. Gerber estimated the body had been dead for over a year, making cause of death or identification unlikely. He noted there was "considerable hacking and cutting of the third, fourth and fifth cervical vertebrae, but the state of decomposition prevented a precise determination of whether or not decapitation was the cause of death." Certain features of the remains led the coroner to conclude the victim was African-American. Despite several tips as to Victim No. 8's identity, it was never determined. The press continued benign reporting of the investigation.

Seemingly in need of more publicity, the Mad Butcher struck again only weeks after the skeletal remains of Victim No. 8 were found. Once again, perhaps to be assured credit for the crime, the Mad Butcher chose Kingsbury Run as his dumping ground. On July 6, 1937, a man's torso and two thighs were found floating in the Cuyahoga River near Kingsbury Run. In the following week, the river yielded most of the victim's remains, excluding the head. Decapitation, the Mad Butcher's calling card, was determined to be the cause of death. The victim was never identified. All that could be determined was that he was a white male, approximate height of five foot eight, weight of 150 pounds, and an age of around forty years. Victim No. 9 joined the growing list of unfortunate lost souls.

Coroner Gerber offered Eliot Ness his opinion that, due to the relatively precise manner in which the bodies were dismembered, the police should consider the perpetrator to be someone with medical skills, such as a physician, medical student, or nurse. The Mad Butcher was also likely a large man capable of carrying the carnage he created long distances. The investigators had very little other information to help them track the Mad Butcher.

With the media agreeing to suppress stories of the serial murderer known as the Mad Butcher of Kingsbury Run, Eliot Ness turned his attention to civil disorders in Cleveland in the summer of 1937 as riots erupted around the Depression-weary city. Although detectives continued to follow any leads, most of which led nowhere, Ness didn't become any more active in the cases.

Detectives worked every angle of the cases, developing several suspects and leads. Nothing had panned out by April 8, 1938, when the severed leg of a woman was fished out of the Cuyahoga River. Ness and the police department hoped the find was not related to the case, guessing the bone fragment and tissue were the result of a boating accident or, at worst, a newly discovered piece of a prior victim. Coroner Gerber announced the find as being "not over two days old." Ness, apparently tiring of the coroner's growing share of publicity surrounding the investigations, demanded an independent examination for evaluation of the time of death. Dr. Gerber steadfastly refused.

The following month, Gerber's finding proved correct. Two burlap bags containing a woman's nude, bisected torso, thighs, and a foot were pulled from the Cuyahoga River: more pieces of Victim No. 10. The autopsy judged the victim to be a white female, between twenty-five and thirty years old, approximately five feet two inches tall and weighing 120 pounds. The coroner also noted "multiple hesitation marks," with lacerations to both thighs, and the fact the killer had broken the victim's back ribs with his bare hands. Victim No. 10 was the first in the series of murders to show evidence of drugs in her system. Enough morphine was detected to have caused unconsciousness or even death. Because of the low amount of blood in her heart, the coroner ruled Victim No. 10's cause of death as "possible laceration anterior aspect neck with secondary hemorrhage." The victim's head, both arms and hands, and right leg and foot were never located.

As in the past, clues to catching the Mad Butcher all seemingly led nowhere. Law enforcement methods in the 1930s relied heavily on eyewitness accounts, interviews and interrogations, assessment of motive, and detective skills. Safety Director Ness couldn't have known the dynamics and forensic technology necessary to apprehend a killer who preyed upon strangers, was highly intelligent, and motivated by a sick psyche few could understand. Public fear over the Mad Butcher's roaming the city was at a fever pitch. Things had quieted down by August 16, 1938, when more body parts turned up at a dump at the end of East Ninth Street.

Dismembered body parts of a female were found by poverty-stricken area residents scouring the dump for anything that might have any value. When news of the find got out, more waves of the curious crowded the surrounding area for a glimpse. One of the onlookers noticed a foul odor emanating from a sunken hole in the earth. Further evaluation revealed another rotting corpse—this one a man.

Were these the Mad Butcher's victims No. 11 and No. 12? Some of the evidence, such as the bodies' location, suggested they were not. Regardless, the citizens of Cleveland believed they were. Criticism and pressure from politicians, the newspapers, and the public at large rained upon Eliot Ness and the police department. His reputation, and indeed ego, on the line, Ness needed a display of results, and he needed them quickly. After conferring with Mayor Burton and senior officers in the police department, Ness had a plan, albeit one that would prove to be a huge error in judgment.

In the late night hours of August 18, 1938, two days after the two bodies were found at the East 9th Street dump, Ness led officers from the Cleveland police force on a midnight raid of the hobo camps and shantytowns behind Public Square. He continued the roust into the Flats area near the Cuyahoga River, then moved into Kingsbury Run. Ness's squad rounded up the startled vagrants, took them to the station house for fingerprinting, then shipped them en masse to the work-house. After searching the area for any clue of the Mad Butcher, Ness ordered the shacks and their contents burned to prevent the residents from returning.

Ness justified the destruction of the shantytowns by claiming to deprive the Mad Butcher of future victims. "Henceforth," he said, "such men will have to stay at the Wayfarer's Lodge, where there are ample facilities for them." The Cleveland newspapers weren't buying it. The *Press* ran several editorials critical of the action: "That such Shantytowns exist is a sorrowful reflection upon the state of society. The throwing into jail of men broken by experience and the burning of their wretched places of habitation will not solve the economic problem. Nor is it likely to lead to the solution of the most macabre mystery in Cleveland's history."

Proving the torching of shantytowns and the "roundup" arrest of its residents wasn't going away, the *Press* continued to fault Ness for the idea in the coming days: "The net result of the director's raid seems to be the wrecking of a few miserable huts and the confinement of the occupants, along with jobless men seized in similar raids, at the Workhouse. As we said a week ago, we can see no justification for the jailing of jobless and penniless men and the wrecking of their miserable hovels without permitting them to collect their personal belongings."

The spotlight was on Ness to arrest the Mad Butcher. The investigation seemed stalled. The public spectacle of the raids had backfired terribly. Several other questionable methods of investigation were attempted, yielding no results.

The Mad Butcher of Kingsbury Run faded from the scene in late 1938. His reasons for halting the vile succession of murders, or simply relocating, remain a mystery. One reason could be that Ness got too close.

One theory identifies Dr. Frank Sweeney, a man who had a rags-to-riches-to-rags life story, as a viable suspect. Sweeney grew up in the Kingsbury Run area in a family affected by poverty. Against the odds, he had managed to put himself through medical school, marry, father two sons, and run a respectable medical practice. He was a veteran of World War I and received a military disability for a head injury or mental illness (the reason is not clear). Dr. Sweeney's life hit the skids when he began drinking too much. His alcoholism led him to

Homeless men fill the jail after being displaced by the burning of the shantytowns.

violence, which eventually led to the disintegration of his marriage and medical practice. Tall and muscular, Sweeney bore the police physical profile of how the Mad Butcher would appear.

On August 23, 1938, Ness arranged for an interview with Dr. Sweeney using a polygraph, a tool brand new to law enforcement and still in the developmental stages. The arrangement was complicated because Sweeney had powerful political connections in his first cousin, Democratic Congressman Martin L. Sweeney, a critic of Eliot Ness. But when the time came, Sweeney submitted to questioning.

Ness arranged for the interview to take place in a suite at the Cleveland Hotel on Public Square. Present with Ness were the court psychiatrist, Dr. Royal Grossman, Police Lieutenant David Cowles, and Dr. Leonard Keeler, one of the inventors of the polygraph who would do the questioning. After several hours of interrogation, Dr. Keeler commented, "Look's like he's your guy." Psychiatrist Grossman agreed, describing Sweeney as a "classic psychopath with the likelihood of some schizophrenia."

Despite the assertions, Frank Sweeney vehemently denied knowledge of the crimes and challenged Safety Director Ness to bring charges. The case against Sweeney remained largely circumstantial. For unknown reasons, perhaps political influence, perhaps lack of evidence, Sweeney was never charged. He checked himself into a mental hospital two days after the interrogation and remained hospitalized, at one facility or another, until his death in 1965.

The serial killings officially stopped in 1938, but that didn't stop Democratic opponents of Republican Mayor Harold Burton and his "hired gun from Washington" from getting involved in an apparent attempt to discredit Ness. Cuyahoga County Sheriff Martin O'Donnell, a leading Democrat, hired a private investigator to look into the Kingsbury Run murders. As a result, the only person ever charged in the slayings was Frank

Dolezal, a drifter who had ancillary links to some of the Mad Butcher's victims. It was suggested Dolezal's "confession" resulted from beatings he took at the hands of sheriff's deputies. As the case against Frank Dolezal disintegrated under scrutiny, he died under suspicious circumstances at the county jail by what the sheriff's office described as "suicide."

In his 2005 book, *Corroborating Evidence: The Black Dahlia Murder,* author William T. Rasmussen links the Kingsbury Run murders to a man named Jack Wilson, a one-time butcher from Cleveland, who became a suspect in the famous "Black Dahlia" dismemberment murder case in Los Angeles, California. Similarities and coincidence in the cases and timeline exist, but nothing to lead to absolute proof.

The identity of the Mad Butcher of Kingsbury Run remains a mystery to this day. Some say Eliot Ness's reputation as a law enforcement officer suffered because of his failure to bring the Mad Butcher of Kingsbury Run to justice. His life as Cleveland's safety director ended with his admission to being involved in a hit-and-run auto accident on a frigid northern Ohio night. Ness lost a run for Cleveland mayor in the 1940s and was involved in private industry but failed to prosper.

He died of an apparent heart attack on May 16, 1957, in Coudersport, Pennsylvania, at the age of fifty-four. The body was cremated, and the ashes sat on a shelf in the garage of a family member's home until 1997, when they were returned to Cleveland and spread on Lake View Cemetery's Wade Lake in a formal ceremony held by the Cleveland Police Department. A marker at the cemetery stands tribute to Ness, his wife, and son.

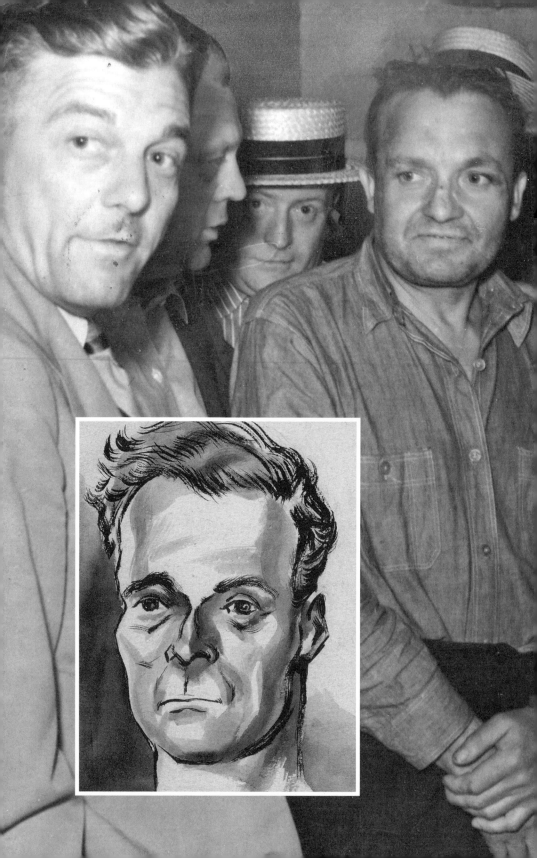

Detectives surround suspect Frank Dolezal, a suspect in the killing spree who bears a resemblance to an artist's rendering of the murderer based on descriptions from various witnesses.

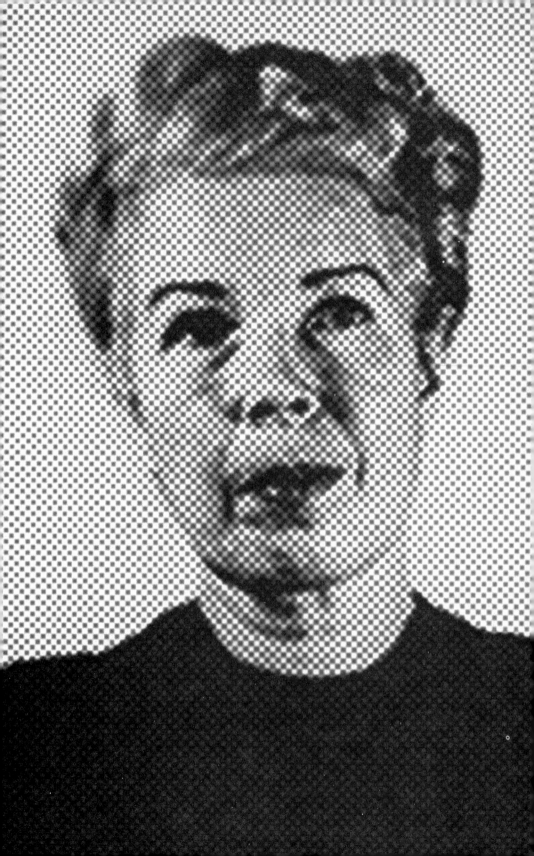

MILDRED

"AXIS SALLY"

GILLARS

On the Air
in
Europe!

6

Der Führer's Favorite Late-Night Radio

WORLD WAR II TOOK MANY SONS AND daughters of Ohio, some of whom found their way to the liberation of Europe and victory over Nazi Germany. Like other wars, too many Ohioans made the ultimate sacrifice and never returned. Many others did come home from the war to resume life in the Midwest. One gal from Conneaut, however, had her trip home from the German front delayed while she spent two years at Alderson Federal Prison in West Virginia for consorting with the Nazis.

Mildred Gillars was born in New England on November 29, 1900. By the time she was a teenager, her family took up residence along the shores of Lake Erie in the northeast Ohio town of Conneaut. An aspiring actress, Mildred studied drama at Ohio Wesleyan University but dropped out short of graduation. By the age of twenty-five, the attractive blonde decided to head to New York and acting fame. A grandmother's will had set up a "to be used for college only" inheritance trust fund for the young beauty, so as she sought a place on the Broadway stage, she enrolled at New York City's Hunter College. It was there she caught the eye of German literature professor Max Otto Koischwitz.

Koischwitz, a dedicated German national with strong sentiment for the fatherland, found Fraulein Gillars, with her statuesque build and flowing blonde hair, very appealing to his Teutonic tastes. After all, at twenty-five, she was older than most of his students and, unlike the typical college kid, she lived in her own off-campus apartment. In short order Professor Koischwitz arranged after-hours tutoring sessions with the young fraulein, presumably for help in her study of German literature, but leading more toward instruction in the social and biological sciences.

Like many other of the professor's students, Mildred Gillars found herself infatuated, even "in love" with Max Koischwitz. She's quoted as saying their liaison "... forever sealed my fate ... that first moment our eyes met. He is ... was ... my destiny." Destiny indeed.

What followed for Herr Professor Koischwitz and the pretty Miss Gillars was several years of secret meetings for sex, broken promises from the professor, and Mildred's realization her love affair amounted to little more than a dead-end street. Mildred eventually discovered her lover's true reason for keeping their relationship a secret. The professor was married to a

German woman, always had been, and the couple parented two daughters, one of whom was born during Mildred and Max's romance. Mildred didn't seem to care. She continued in the affair until Koischwitz couldn't take the pressure, perhaps from conscience but more likely from fear of losing his job if his involvement with a student was discovered. He dumped her. Blaming her inability to forget Max Otto Koischwitz in the years to come, Mildred Gillars credits a broken heart with her transition from Ohio girl to the reputed Nazi sweetheart radio broadcaster Axis Sally.

Another attempt at acting failed, while Mildred Gillars began and ended a series of relationships with different men. She even acted as the female companion "cover" for a homosexual. She traveled widely, living in New York, Algiers, Paris, and Washington, D.C. During the height of the Great Depression, Gillars returned to Conneaut for a while. What she found there didn't suit her now more Eastern tastes. Like most in the United States, Ohio cities suffered hard times during the 1930s and Conneaut was no exception. Where banks, department stores, and restaurants once stood, Mildred found buildings with repossession notices plastered on boarded-up windows and doors.

The drudgery of "hard times" in Ohio made Mildred jump at the chance to reignite the flame of romance with an old suitor who happened to be a British diplomat living in Algiers. The man, Charles Dunsworthy, provided cash and a steamship ticket to get Miss Gillars by his side. Dunsworthy did everything he could to persuade Mildred to become his wife, but Mildred's long-standing devotion to Max Koischwitz held its grip. Within months she left Dunsworthy and began a stopgap tour of Europe, taking on jobs here and there and ending up in 1939 in what had become the center of Nazi Germany.

Berlin brought ample opportunities for Mildred Gillars in

Adolf Hitler attracted many followers, including
Mildred Gillars lover Max Koischwitz

"The Bitch of Berlin"

Mildred Gillars

several ways. First and foremost, Max Otto Koischwitz was back in his hometown. The former professor returned to Deutschland shortly after the invasion of France. Koischwitz would use his experience in America to work at the Reichrundfunk, the Nazi propaganda radio station run by later-convicted war criminal Doctor Joseph Goebbels. He portrayed "The Professor," a radio program character designed to sway America's youth toward Nazi favor in a broadcast called *The College Hour.*

Fraulein Gillars, who by now also was in Goebbels's employ, took advantage of circumstances and took up exactly where she left off with Max. Their affair resumed and, despite what Gillars said was a "performance" put on under Gestapo

"Hello, boys, this is

duress, "Axis Sally" was born to the worldwide radio audience. The broadcasts were strictly monitored and scripted by the Gestapo, sometimes poorly written but read verbatim. For example: "Shame on those who spread lies about the Vaterland! Do not believe here shortages exist! Stocked good are our stores. Germans eat three meals good every day while in England you for miles for one cup of tea line up. Shame on Queen Wilhelmina, just because your Netherlands surrendered to the Führer you did not have to England run off!"

By 1943 Mildred had become "Midge at the Microphone" cooing in a sultry voice with bits like: "Hello, boys, this is Gerry's front calling. This program is specially dedicated to Uncle Sam's boys and goes out on the air every night from 6:30 p.m. to 7:30 p.m. on the meeting way at 221 and 391 and shortwave at 28 and 39.45." Midge's broadcast also featured American popular music performed by German bands like Bruno and His Swinging Tigers, an ensemble made up of prisoners of the Reich, some of whom were jailed for playing swing music in the first place. Midge would intersperse the program with messages "calculated to nauseate you [GIs] with nostalgia. Stay tuned for sentimental tunes straight from Tin Pan Alley— all selected to make you homesick for your two-timing wives and sweethearts."

Whether American soldiers were affected by "Axis Sally," a name they had given her, is debatable. What is certain is most U.S. troops recognized Sally's voice and listened to her broadcasts. Some say Axis Sally was more entertaining than anything

Gerry's front calling."

else even when she said things like, "Well boys, how are my sweethearts tonight? Comfy? Feeling like cuddling up to that special, soft, and sweet someone? Dying to hold her in your big, powerful arms? You may dislike my repeating this to you, but let's face it, you may get mutilated and not return home in one piece. Now, you know how your girl wants her man. Suppose she'll settle for damaged goods?"

Stabs at nostalgia weren't Axis Sally's only trick. She tried to scare the troops by appearing "omnipresent," as in this broadcast of information garnered from Nazi intelligence reports aimed at American soldiers in combat in Italy: "Hi, fellas. I see you synchronizing your watches against the clock in the village square. Yes, you heard me right, Private Jimmy Zonski from Oxnard, California. You are the son of Judy

Zonski. How's her oil painting coming along? And I see you synchronizing your watch, Sergeant Bill Smiting, brother of the former linebacker for the Buckeyes. Well, enough chitchat."

Besides playing "big sister" to troops in the field, "The Bitch of Berlin" also made a whirlwind of the prison camps where Allied soldiers were held. She recorded interviews with the POWs for play on her show. She taunted her audience by broadcasting the names, hometowns, and names of next of kin of servicemen who had been recently taken prisoner.

Axis Sally broadcast her most infamous program on May 11, 1944, a little less than a month prior to the D-Day Normandy invasion. With Germany anticipating a major Allied assault, Max Koischwitz received permission from German propagandists to write *Vision of the Invasion*, a play designed to make Allied soldiers turn back from any invasion of France. Mildred portrayed the mother of an American soldier. The mother dreams a vision of her son meeting a violent death in the English Channel: "Please, please, my son, I beg of you … your mother is on her knees begging you … do not take part in this invasion, this trap. Please don't, I can't bear it! Don't pierce my heart with the grief of losing you! To challenge those German fortifications above those beaches is to die a horrible death. … It will be a slaughter, my darling, the worst slaughter in history. … Please, while there's still time, please my precious son, lay down your arms. Lay down your arms and come home." The announcer's line made the message clear: "The D of D-Day stands for DOOM—Disaster—Death—Defeat—Dunkirk or Dieppe."

History shows Axis Sally's impact, if there was any, over D-Day or the outcome of World War II. The Allies prevailed, forcing Germany to capitulate. By all accounts, Mildred Gillars's final years in Germany proved dismal. Max Koischwitz committed suicide shortly before Germany's official surrender, leaving his "Liebling" to fend for herself in the aftermath. The GIs' "Gal Sal" used aliases and meandered around bombed-out Berlin, joining the ranks of the displaced and homeless. She was arrested by the U.S. Army in 1948 and returned to the United States to face multiple charges of treason.

On March 8, 1949, after a six-week trial and long deliberations, Mildred Gillars, aka Axis Sally, was convicted of one count of treason against the United States of America for portraying an American soldier's mother in *Vision of the Invasion*. She was sentenced to ten to thirty years' imprisonment. She remained in West Virginia's Alderson Federal Prison until she was granted parole in 1962.

From there, Mildred Gillars finally returned to her home state of Ohio, where she moved to an apartment on the north side of Columbus. There she took a job teaching music to kindergartners at Our Lady of Bethlehem Catholic School. In 1973, she returned to Ohio Wesleyan University, where she earned a bachelor's degree in speech and was deemed "the oldest person ever to graduate from Ohio Wesleyan."

Mildred Gillars died of natural causes on June 1, 1988, at the age of eighty-seven. She is buried at St. Joseph's Cemetery in Columbus, Ohio.

AXIS SALLY

CALL-BULLETIN

Mildred Gillars as she looked at her arrest for treason (above)
and as a kindergarten music teacher (right).

DONALD MARTIN

The Murder **Mystery** of a Cincinnati Police Officer

7

A Very Cold Case

Donald Martin

ON THE WALL OF THE MAIN AUDITORIUM AT the Cincinnati Police Academy in Lower Price Hill hangs a line of photos depicting a morbid fraternity. Portraits of officers slain in the line of duty cast watchful eyes over the new recruits as they prepare to take their places in the thin blue line. It was the same in 1981, when I entered the academy. Our instructors explained the purpose of the photographs. Study the facts surrounding each officer's death, we were told. Learn from these tragedies.

Then, as now, the first photo in the lineup was a picture of a handsome young man with dark hair topped with a white police cap. His face bears an affable smile under kind brown eyes open wide with apparent anticipation. His name was Donald Martin. As a young recruit, I found Martin's photograph far more disturbing than any of the others. The details of each officer's slaying and the conclusion of each case accompanied all the other photos; only Martin's murder was unsolved. It stayed that way until 2005.

In February 2005, two homicide detectives pulled the Martin file from cold-case storage. There are, of course, remarkable forensic tools not available to law enforcement in 1961 that sometimes help investigators solve cold cases today. But this forty-four-year-old mystery did not give up its secrets easily. So the officers took a journey into the past, re-creating a murder scene that has long since disappeared, retracing the footsteps (and missteps) of a dormant investigation, and probing a family's dark history. In the end, they solved the murder of Donald Martin—a crime committed before they were born.

On the evening of March 10, 1961, Patrolman Donald Martin was excited when he reported to work. Life was changing for the twenty-nine-year-old west sider. That winter, Martin and his wife, Gail, had applied to become adoptive parents through the Protestant Orphan Home. Now the two had great news: They were getting a baby.

Adding a child to the family would require a larger car, which is why Martin asked his supervisor, Sergeant Hike Bogosian, if he could visit some of the car lots on his beat if the night proved quiet. Sergeant Bogosian gave his permission. He knew that Martin's presence on the neighborhood's car lots meant he'd be doing extra security checks at the same time— all the better for local businesses. Martin's beat was the

Pendleton neighborhood, which lies along Reading Road northeast of downtown. Back then, I-71 was nonexistent, railroad tracks ran where the expressway stands today, and Reading Road was a major thoroughfare into the city. It was a good place to have an upscale auto dealership, and one of the businesses located there was Downtown Lincoln-Mercury Auto Sales.

At around 3 a.m., Martin notified the police dispatcher from his in-car radio that he was out of the cruiser checking the southern end of Reading Road near downtown. Today there's a Staples office supply store and the I-471 entrance ramp on the east side of the road; in 1961 the block held the National Biscuit Company (Nabisco) building at 721 Reading, the Lincoln-Mercury dealership at 715, and a vacant lot in between. That's where the mystery began.

Just minutes after Martin's call to the dispatcher, a carload of young men, returning home from a night of gambling in Newport, Kentucky, witnessed an event that would haunt them for years. "We were in my friend's car. I was on the passenger side in the back when we heard a couple of shots, two or three, I don't remember," says Harold Stiver, one of the witnesses. "I remember the guy standing behind the officer when I first spotted him. The officer had his hands up in the air like he was begging for his life, and the guy lowered the gun at full arm's length, point-blank range, and shot him."

Shocked, the young men turned the car around to help the fallen patrolman. "He [the suspect] fired a shot toward us that went through the back window of a car close to where we were," Stiver remembers. "I jumped out and flagged down a police car that was coming by."

According to one of the officers on the scene, Martin muttered a few words, but the only thing the officer could understand was, "I've had it." Martin was admitted to General

Hospital (now University Hospital) with multiple gunshot wounds at 3:19 a.m. and rushed into surgery. At 5 a.m., almost two hours into the operation, the surgeon pronounced Donald Martin dead.

Harold Stiver, now sixty-nine, retired, and living in Florida, still pities the police officer he saw brutally murdered so long ago. "It wasn't like it was a gunfight or anything," he says. "It was cold-blooded."

Donald Martin was born in Kentucky on May 4, 1931, to Claude and Allie Martin. He attended the Ohio Mechanic's Institute, then enlisted in the Army in 1948. He served in the First Cavalry Division in Tokyo, Japan, followed by twelve months of combat duty in Korea, earning the rank of corporal, the Korean Service Medal, and three Bronze Stars. Discharge came in 1952. Four years later, he became Patrolman Don Martin. According to his application to join the police department, he was a shade under six feet and a shade over 200 pounds, and he enjoyed baseball, swimming, reading, and "working around the house." Martin found his calling with the police department. "He was just a great, clean-cut guy, a real team worker who always got the job done with no excuses," says eighty-six-year-old Hike Bogosian, who was Martin's immediate supervisor. "Don ran a tough beat [and] he was a good policeman. You wished you would have had eight or ten like him."

Don and Gail Martin married in 1954 and bought a home on Foley Road, a quiet Price Hill street. By the spring of 1961, Gail had resigned her job—she was secretary to Chief of Detectives Lieutenant Colonel Henry Sandman—in anticipation of becoming a full-time mother.

The handsome young officer had endeared himself to neighbors. "He was king of the neighborhood," says Bob Ellerman, then the Martins' eight-year-old neighbor. "He always had a

The Lincoln-Mercury dealership on Reading Road that was the scene of Patrolman Martin's brutal murder. (inset) Aerial view of the dealership.

smile on his face; he'd take the time to do things like throw ball with us, and he was always playing pranks on us. I remember how excited he was to be adopting a baby. He'd shown us kids the nursery he and his wife had prepared."

Martin appeared on the Ellermans' front porch before leaving for work on March 10. "He said he had good news," says Gene Ellerman, Bob's father. "He said, 'We're bringing the baby home next week.' " The elder Ellerman offered congratulations and suggested they have a drink to celebrate. "No," Ellerman says Martin told him, "I have to work tonight, but I'll have a Coke." It was the last time the Ellerman family saw him alive.

By sunrise on March 11, teams of officers were combing every inch of the car dealership and surrounding area for clues. The department poured every available resource into the investigation, and scores of off-duty officers joined in. The lot where the killing occurred yielded evidence of a violent struggle between Martin and his assailant. A copper Cincinnati Police uniform button, torn from the officer's jacket, was found where police believed the confrontation began. Near it was an ordinary white button, assumed to be the perpetrator's. There was a red thread hanging from it—a clue that eventually pointed to the gunman's escape route. Based on the witness's account, the location of the torn-away buttons, and the spot where Martin was found, investigators surmised Martin encountered the perpetrator on the car lot. A struggle ensued, and the officer was somehow disarmed and shot three times with his own revolver. Martin was trying to make it to his vehicle to call for help when he was shot again in the head behind his left ear.

Northwest of the scene, in Mt. Auburn, on a street made up mostly of five-story apartment buildings, the "big break" seemed to come. In the alley behind 542 Dandridge, a patrolman spotted the butt end of Martin's revolver sticking out of a

(left) Patrolman Martin's uniform coat with the bullet holes and missing top gold button. (below) The garbage can where Martin's service revolver was discovered. (below left) The bullet-shattered rear window of a car parked on Reading Road. Walls hit the car while firing at the witnesses.

garbage can. Detectives converged on the alley. Going through more garbage cans, they found a gray jacket and a red-and-white flannel shirt wrapped in a white pillowcase and covered with trash. The shirt was minus one white button. "When we find the owner of the shirt and jacket," Chief of Detectives Henry Sandman told reporters, "we'll have the killer."

Police followed up on scores of tips and clues. Investigators checked the tags in the shirt and pillowcase, trying to narrow the search to patrons of a specific dry cleaner or clothing store, but that proved fruitless. An FBI analysis of hairs found in the shirt pocket only confused matters. The FBI said the hairs belonged to an African-American; the car full of witnesses clearly described a white suspect. Police flooded the city with fliers containing information on the crime and photographs of the killer's jacket and shirt in hopes a citizen could match the clothing to an individual. Nothing significant came to light.

Martin's funeral was held at Concordia Lutheran Church at 1524 Race Street in Over-the-Rhine on March 14, 1961. The *Times Star* quoted the eulogy offered by the Reverend Arthur Scheidt: "This was no monster who committed this crime," he said. "It was a man. One of us here might be a friend or relative of the man who stooped so low as to commit this crime which so tragically ended the life of Don Martin." His tribute might have been interpreted as an entreaty for one of those friends or relatives to come forward with information. But no one did.

Days turned into months and, eventually, to years. Lt. Colonel Sandman even sought help from true crime magazines—one way to reach crime-curious citizens back in the days before television shows like *America's Most Wanted*. In the August 1963 issue of *True Detective Magazine*, Sandman was quoted as saying, "The Patrolman Donald Martin case is over two years old. Hundreds of leads have been followed without success. This case, like all other unsolved murders, will remain active and any new leads will be vigorously pursued. The best hope for the apprehension of Patrolman Martin's killer is some information not yet revealed to our police department." He then asked the magazine's readers for any leads or information they could provide.

In 1965, the Martin killing officially became a cold case with the death of a man many in the homicide squad believed was responsible for the murder. Records from the investigation eventually were moved into the cold-case file catacombs locked deep in the basement of Cincinnati Police District Four in North Avondale. But even though the file was out of sight, the murder took on a life of its own, achieving folklore status within the department. Speculation and stories were passed from generation to generation. The most persistent of these was that the killer was a criminal named Frank Murph. The theory was born in April 1961, when an anonymous source mailed a newspaper article from the *Cincinnati Enquirer* with a note that suggested police look at Murph for the Martin murder. The article reported that Murph, thirty, of Mt. Auburn, had been sentenced to nine months in the Workhouse and a $900 fine for violently resisting arrest when caught shoplifting from the Kroger store on Madison Road. It was the last sentence of the article that got everyone's attention: "Murph was arrested after a struggle in which he disarmed Patrolman Raymond Davis."

Murph as a suspect must have seemed to make sense. He'd tried to disarm another officer, and he lived in the neighborhood where Martin was shot. The story that circulated among officers was that Murph was black but light-skinned, which could have explained the discrepancy between the hair samples in the shirt pocket and the witnesses' descriptions.

In reality, Homicide Lt. Charles Martin (no relation to Donald) had investigated the Frank Murph lead right after Murph's arrest a month and a day away from the Martin murder on April 12, 1961. What he found was that Murph couldn't have killed the officer because he was in jail when it happened. Lt. Martin noted his findings in the ever-growing mound of paperwork generated by the Martin case, but because he died suddenly in 1962, he wasn't around to set people straight when Murph's name was repeatedly added to the Martin murder legend. So, to most police officers, Frank Murph remained a likely suspect—especially after 1965, when he was shot and killed trying to disarm a police officer after a botched robbery in Ft. Wayne, Indiana.

There were other theories and speculation about Donald Martin's murder, but nothing was ever substantiated. The lack of closure seemed to leave a frustrated hollowness in officers of every generation.

Detectives Jeff Schare and Kurt Ballman happened to be on duty in February 2005 when a small, fragile-looking woman came to the homicide squad at Criminal Investigation Section headquarters at 824 Broadway with a disturbing story. The woman's health was failing, and she told the detectives she needed to ease her conscience about something her former husband said four decades ago. She was a young bride back then—a newlywed who quickly discovered her husband to be a violent alcoholic. She learned to fear the man's drunken rages, a fact that was magnified one night when, during a whiskey-induced rant, he told the tale of how he had "once shot a cop."

Schare and Ballman listened intently as the woman related how her now ex-husband said that he and an accomplice were breaking into a train car in a Cincinnati railroad yard when they were confronted by "a figure in the shadows." Assuming they were caught by a police officer, both men pulled pistols and fired, shooting the victim. "If you ever tell anyone, I'll fucking kill you!" he told the terrified woman. The threat had silenced her for years.

The woman said she'd been married in 1963, and she thought the incident had occurred a few years before that. Even though Donald Martin had died before they were born, the detectives had heard the stories about his murder and went in search of the file. "If God had a hand in it, if there was divine intervention, this was it," says Ballman. "The first box we looked in was marked 'miscellaneous homicides.' The first file we pulled read 'Patrolman Donald Martin Homicide.' "

Reviewing the details, they quickly realized that the aging woman's confessional was not about the Martin case, and they could find no record of similar unsolved crimes in the area in the early 1960s. It appeared that the husband's drunken tale was just that—a fabrication. But for detectives Schare and Ballman, it was the beginning of a new investigation—one they were going to own. "When we were going through the evidence," recalls Ballman, "I pulled out Don's uniform and police hat and realized it's the same kind we wear today. I got teary-eyed. I knew we had to give it a shot."

Schare and Ballman have a lot in common. Partners on the homicide squad for four years, both were born in May 1963, both graduated from the same police academy class fifteen years ago, both hold advanced degrees from the University of Cincinnati, both are experts in the martial arts, and both "hate to lose," says Schare. That's where the similarities end. Kurt Ballman stands six foot five with muscular girth to match. He has an easy smile and is not afraid to share his emotions. At five foot six, Jeff Schare is compact and wiry. Schare's businesslike demeanor belies the nickname "Pee Wee" (as in Pee Wee Herman) given to him by coworkers who've noticed a marked similarity to the comedian. For these detectives, "giving it a shot" meant starting from scratch. Simply going through the file alerted them to holes in the Martin lore. For one thing, they realized that, despite all the stories, Frank Murph had been cleared four decades ago. "Once we destroyed the myth that it wasn't the person everybody assumed," says Schare, "it gave us the resolve to believe we could solve this case."

They ignored hearsay; they also reconsidered previous leads that had been labeled dead ends. They examined every piece of evidence and every shred of documentation they could find and turned to forensic tools developed since the early 1960s. Still, a cutting-edge technique for recovering fingerprints on fabric failed to produce anything usable from Martin's uniform jacket; even the new "super glue" fingerprint process—in which glue is vaporized and applied to metal—failed to retrieve anything definitive from the murder weapon.

This was the first cold case either had ever worked, and it was frustrating. "One of the things about being a homicide detective [is] you always want to go to the scene," Ballman says. "Being that the scene in this case is completely changed, we just couldn't get a feel for it. That's when Jeff got the idea to find retired detectives who had actually worked the case."

Now seventy-four years old, Jerry Schimpf was a young detective working out of the Juvenile Bureau in 1962, almost a year after Don Martin's murder. Schimpf was eating at a downtown diner when he noticed a group of young men come in and take a table. He recognized one of them as the brother of the suspect in a rape case he was working. Schimpf made his way over and sat down at the group's table, asking the brother about the rape suspect's whereabouts. The brother decided to play tough. "You think you can take all of us?" he sneered.

"I don't know," answered Schimpf, "but you better look under the table. You're first."

The kid glanced under the table and, upon noticing Schimpf's pistol pointed in his direction, decided to change his tack. "Do you think you can help my brother out if I give you the name of a cop killer?" he bargained.

Walter Baker Walls was the name Schimpf received. Walls, a twenty-nine-year-old who lived in Over-the-Rhine, had a long criminal record and a propensity for tough talk. He told one girlfriend that he was a member of "Satan's Disciples," a motorcycle gang with a bad reputation, and he bragged to friends and family that he had ties to organized crime in Newport.

Schimpf took Walls's name to Detective Chief Henry Sandman. Sandman in turn assigned Schimpf to work on the case with veteran homicide detective Will "Staggie" Stagenhorst. Stagenhorst and Schimpf traveled to the Ohio State Penitentiary in Columbus, where Walter Walls was serving time for a parole violation from a burglary conviction. Short and stocky with slicked-back black hair, Walls looked remarkably similar to the police artist's sketch of the murderer drawn from descriptions provided by Harold Stiver and the other three witnesses. So similar, in fact, the detective's next move was to bring Stiver and his friends to the Ohio Penitentiary for a positive identification. "He sure looked like the guy," Stiver remembers. "I just couldn't be a hundred percent sure." The abandoned clothing also fit Walls, who persistently denied knowledge of the crime. Walls agreed to a lie detector test, which, according to Schimpf, he "failed miserably." But that's where the investigation stalled. "Will Stagenhorst was convinced it was Walter Walls, but didn't have enough back then to prove it," says Schare. "They just didn't have any solid physical evidence, the witnesses weren't a hundred percent sure, and nobody in the Walls family would talk for fear of Walter."

Time passed, and no charges were brought. Jerry Schimpf left the police department in 1967 and became an attorney. Will Stagenhorst retired from police work in May 1965 and died in 1992.

Ballman and Schare had the Martin case file, but the file Schimpf and Stagenhorst had kept on Walls was missing. They speculate that Stagenhorst took the Walls file with him for safe-keeping when he retired. That wasn't unusual at the time; often detectives felt protective of unsolved cases and wanted their records where they would not be lost. Ironically, that's exactly what Schare and Ballman think happened when Stagenhorst died—the file was probably discarded, and with it, the history of Wells as a suspect.

Today Jerry Schimpf can't explain why Walter Walls's name

"This isn't about my

didn't attach itself to the department's chatter about the murder in the 1960s. "I think it kind of fell through the cracks when Staggie [Will Stagenhorst] retired," he says now. For years, apparently satisfied with the story of Frank Murph, no one knew to associate Walls with the case. The job for Schare and Ballman, then, was to find all the bits that "fell through the cracks" and piece together the puzzle.

Released from prison in 1963, Walter Baker Walls continued life on the fringes of the criminal justice system, including involvement in the 1969 murder of his wife, Anna Walls, at the hands of his girlfriend, Brenda Anders. He died of cancer in 2002, but not before leaving a legacy of threats and violence.

Schare and Ballman identified and tracked down anyone they could associate with the case—family members, associates and any police officers and witnesses who might know anything. Their very first interview was with Walter Walls's daughter, Anna Dove. It was an auspicious beginning. When the detectives identified themselves and asked if they could take a moment of her time, Dove immediately blurted out, "This isn't about my dad killing a cop, is it?"

Dove told Schare and Ballman that she was a teenager when Brenda Anders shot her mother. Dove was there when it happened, and as a witness to the murder, she became the object of her father's wrath because he feared her testimony in court. Dove told Schare and Ballman of an encounter where Walls grabbed her, pulled her down an alley, held a handgun to her

dad killing a cop, is it?"

head, and said, "I'll fucking kill you just like I killed that cop!"

The two detectives worked their way through interviews with the rest of Walter Walls's children and other family members. No longer cowed by the violent man, they recounted how, through the years, Walter often bragged that he had "killed a cop." William Walls, Walter's brother, told Ballman and Schare that Walter told him he was trying to break into a car on a dealership lot to steal a battery when he was confronted by a police officer. Walter told William he was able to get the officer's gun and shoot him. William also claimed Walter said that when it happened, he was with another Walls brother and an associate nicknamed "Cadillac Charlie." Walter later told William, "You won't be seeing him anymore. He's in a shallow grave."

(above) Police sketch artist renderings of the suspects.

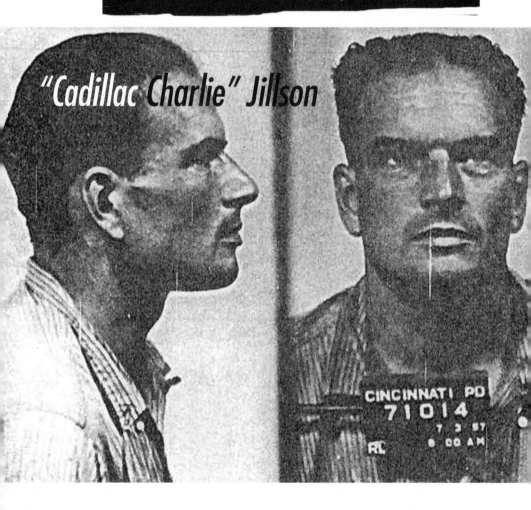

"Cadillac Charlie" Jillson

CINCINNATI PD
71014

The Killers

Walter Walls

CINCINNATI PD
6 2 5 6 2

HK   10 11 83

Eventually the two detectives tracked down Brenda Anders, Walter Walls's onetime girlfriend, who had served eight years in the Ohio Women's Reformatory in Marysville for the murder of Anna Walls. Anders recalled Walter talking about killing a cop. She told them that he even pointed to a particular house on River Road, identifying it as the place where he murdered "Cadillac Charlie" because he was an eyewitness to the killing. Brenda and Walter parted ways when she was convicted of the murder of Walter's wife, Anna Walls, in 1969. Initially charged with complicity to murder, Walter avoided jail by agreeing to testify for the prosecution. "This man just totally had me hypnotized or something," Anders told Detective Schare. "I went there to do it (kill Anna Walls), but I was young and innocent. I'd never shot a gun in my life. I'll never believe I killed her, I think he (Walter) did it, I just took the fall for it. He told me if I confessed it would spare him because I'd never been in trouble. The psychiatrist and all said that he totally had me brainwashed."

In the end, Ballman and Schare determined Walls and two accomplices—his brother Jesse James Walls and Charles "Cadillac Charlie" Jillson—were responsible for the murder of Donald Martin during the early-morning hours of March 11, 1961. Here's the scenario they pieced together:

While Donald Martin worked his shift, brothers Walter and Jesse James Walls of Lower Price Hill were at Ozzie's, a bar at the corner of 13th Street and Reading Road. They were walking that night because neither had a car in running condition. To remedy the situation, Walter called his friend "Cadillac Charlie" Jillson, who lived in Covington, Kentucky, for a ride. Jillson picked up the brothers, and Walter suggested driving around downtown to see if he could locate a suitable car battery to steal. The trio decided to try the Downtown Lincoln-Mercury dealership. Walter got out of the car and headed onto the lot. Jesse stood on the sidewalk as a lookout while Cadillac Charlie waited in his car. Walter found a vehicle with a battery he wanted. He popped the hood and started to remove it.

Around 3 a.m., Don Martin pulled his patrol car into the Nabisco parking lot next door to Downtown Lincoln-Mercury. He walked up a ramp onto the car lot, browsing the available automobiles. When he saw Walter Walls tampering with a vehicle, he confronted him. Walls became violent, and a fight ensued. Martin was wearing his uniform cross-draw holster with his issued .38 caliber revolver. In this close-quarter struggle, Martin had to reach across his abdomen to get at the firearm. But the pistol was already near Walls's right hand, making it easy for him to seize. Martin assuredly felt the chill every cop fears—the criminal had the drop on him. Walls grabbed the gun and shot Martin in the chest. Wounded, Martin turned and ran for the police cruiser. Walls pursued, shooting him twice more in the back. The officer faltered, his knees buckled, and he began to fall to the ground. Walls caught up and, execution style, delivered a fourth shot to the back of Martin's head. Right about then, Walls noticed a car on Reading Road slow down to get a view of the scene. Cadillac Charlie was nowhere to be found; he apparently left in a panic. Walls felt trapped and fired a shot at the witnesses' vehicle, blowing the rear window out of a parked car. The witnesses slowly proceeded up Reading Road and turned around to go back to the fallen officer. Walter Walls ran across Reading Road and up some pedestrian steps to Dandridge Street, where he dumped his clothing and Martin's revolver into trash cans. By now the four witnesses were at the scene, where they saw Jesse Walls, who had come over to look at the mortally wounded officer. Jesse ran east through the Nabisco lot toward the railroad tracks.

In his official review of the Donald Martin homicide investigation, Hamilton County Prosecutor Joe Deters writes, "… based on the statement of the surviving eyewitness to the shooting, as well as statements made to family members of Walter Walls over the years, there is a reasonable likelihood of a conviction for aggravated murder against Walter Walls were this evidence presented to a jury. Since Walter Walls died in 2002, we are unable to bring him to justice for this senseless and brutal crime. Were Walls still alive, I would certainly ask that you file an aggravated murder charge against him. Although we cannot bring criminal charges against Walls, I hope your investigation … brings some sense of closure to the family of Patrolman Martin."

Gail Martin eventually remarried and left Cincinnati. Late in 2005 Police Chief Tom Streicher located her to tell of the news. "There's no doubt that this helped her healing process after forty years," Streicher says. "It was obvious to me that this offered her some sense of comfort, that finally there was closure to a very difficult part of her life." Schare and Ballman are still on the force and have received much-deserved recognition for closing the Martin case.

Donald Martin lies in a neatly manicured section of Arlington Memorial Gardens in Springfield Township. He is surrounded by his mother and other family in a plot beneath a mature black walnut tree, probably only a sapling when he was interred there. His headstone carries a brass disc bearing the seal of the Fraternal Order of Police, and upon it the motto "Justidus / Libertatum"—"Justice and Liberty."

Were justice and liberty served too late for Don Martin? Perhaps not. Streicher says that Martin's case suggests there can be a lot of value in examining a suspect's family lore, even when a case has been unsolved for generations. He's presenting the Martin investigation to the Major City Police Chiefs' Association as an example of a new approach to cold case investigation. "If it provides dividends somewhere around the country, then he really didn't die in vain," Streicher says. "Maybe it's Don Martin's contribution to policing and society some forty-plus years later."

Kurt Ballman and Jeff Schare take pride in closing the forty-four-year-old murder case of a brother officer. Their only regret is the lack of the final "piece of the puzzle" every detective works toward—a judge and jury announcing "guilty" face-to-face with, in this case, a person who affected dozens of lives by senselessly murdering a Cincinnati watchman in 1961.

GOVERNOR JAMES RHODES

Raises Eyebrows!

8

Love Letters from Prison, Big Money, and Four Dead in Ohio

JAMES RHODES SPENT MOST OF HIS ADULT life in Ohio politics. Arguably one of the most powerful men in the state in his time, Rhodes started his political career in 1933 when he was elected Republican committeeman from Columbus. A high school graduate who never bothered with college, Rhodes was elected to four terms as mayor of Columbus and ten years as Ohio State Auditor before being elected governor in 1962. Although prominent in the Republican Party and Ohio politics, Rhodes didn't hit the national radar until *Life* magazine

The capitol building in Columbus

ran a rather scathing story in 1969 alleging ties between the governor's office and Ohio mafia bosses. The story of Jim Rhodes's link to convicted murderer and reputed organized crime kingpin Yonnie Licavoli raised eyebrows all over the Buckeye State.

On the far end of the Prohibition era, an aspiring hoodlum named Thomas "Yonnie" Licavoli rolled into Toledo and quickly opened gambling spots, began a bootlegging operation and started-ed his own series of distilleries. As the operation grew, Licavoli's crew expanded throughout northern Ohio, muscling dry cleaners for "protection," and horning in on competing speakeasy and gambling interests. The takeover soon became bloody.

Governor Martin Davey

On March 8, 1934, a grand jury issued an indictment charging Yonnie Licavoli and twelve others with murdering and conspiring to murder a popular Toledo-area bootlegger named Jackie Kennedy, his girlfriend, and two competing gamblers. Yonnie and four of his henchmen were eventually convicted for the killings and each sentenced to life in an Ohio penitentiary.

That didn't stop Yonnie from remaining northern Ohio's preeminent mob boss. After only two months in prison, there was enough evidence of Yonnie still running his operation from the inside and receiving special favors from prison officials that Governor Martin Davey fired Warden Preston Thomas, a twenty-one-year veteran of the job. Thomas was only the first of three successive wardens to be sacked following charges like permitting known criminals to visit Yonnie Licavoli. Among the prominent "visitors" was Michael DeAngelo, the Columbus Mafia leader, who had a long arrest record and had done three years in a federal penitentiary for conspiracy. The prison visit was the first time investigators could prove a connection between Licavoli and DeAngelo.

Four years later, Warden James Woodard also lost his job for showing special favors to Yonnie Licavoli. By this time, however, Yonnie was well established as the boss on the inside and had set up an internal numbers game and a thriving narcotics and liquor operation.

Even after Licavoli's transfer to the prison system's Hocking Honor Camp near Logan, a 1958 investigation by the Ohio State Highway Patrol led to the dismissal of camp superintendent Lt. Thomas Crowe for accepting "a few presents" from friends of Licavoli. Crowe was even a guest at the luxurious Detroit wedding of Yonnie's daughter. A long Licavoli guest list at the camp included Teamster President James R. Hoffa. A "spring Yonnie" fund of $250,000 was allegedly common knowledge among authorities for years, purportedly offered to several persons of influence, including former Ohio Governor Michael DiSalle. So a shock wave went out across the country when Governor Rhodes announced on January 27, 1969, he had commuted Yonnie Licavoli's sentence from first- to second-

Former governor Michael DiSalle

degree murder, making him eligible for immediate parole.

Life quoted the lead investigator on organized crime in Michigan and northern Ohio, Vincent Piersante, on the possible repercussions of such an action:

This is no ordinary prisoner. The mob in this area needs a shot in the arm. We've been hitting them at the management level and they're feeling it. We are beginning to get witnesses, even some from the Mob's own community. If Yonnie comes out, it will be a feather of every Don in Detroit—especially Pete (Licavoli), who is already too strong. And Yonnie? Yonnie Licavoli has nowhere to go but the Mob. He wouldn't want to go anywhere else.

Despite the noise, Rhodes let the commutation stand. He even filed a defamation lawsuit against *Life* magazine for its "Governor and the Mobster" article (the suit was quietly dropped in 1971). Yonnie Licavoli won parole in early 1971. He died of cancer in 1973 at his daughter's home in Gahanna, Ohio. He is buried at Detroit's Mount Cisco Cemetery.

An interesting, if not ironic, footnote to the Licavoli story can be found in the foreword to Kenneth R. Dickson's book on "Prohibition and murder on Toledo's mean streets," *Nothing Personal Just Business*. Foreword writer and Licavoli murder victim's son Jack Kennedy, Jr., tells of a chance meeting with a former Licavoli gang member who told him, "We liked your father, and that it wasn't personal but business is business."

Not long after the Licavoli controversy, Governor Rhodes found himself at the center of another violent nightmare. A little over a year after "The Governor and the Mobster" was published, James Rhodes was at an Ohio university for a low point in state history, the tragedy some describe as the "Kent State Massacre." No definitive proof of anyone's responsibility for the shooting death of four and wounding of nine on the Kent State University campus in Kent on May 4, 1970, has ever been established. But Governor James Rhodes's political affiliations, coupled with an impassioned speech, have given rise to

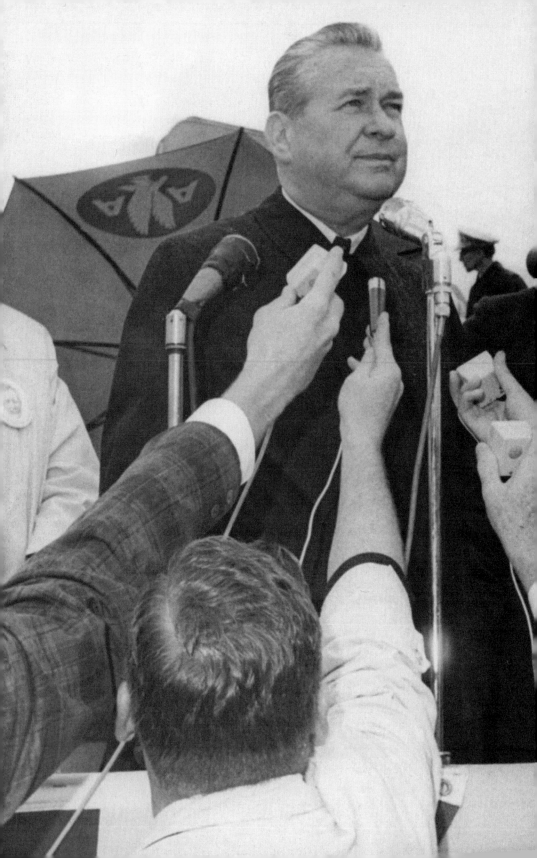

Governor James Rhodes at a press conference in 1965 at Hopkins Airport in Cleveland. To his right is Robert Manry, a Cleveland resident who that year had crossed the Atlantic Ocean in a thirteen-foot sailboat.

theories placing the governor at the heart of the massacre.

After two days of protests and unrest, including the burning of the Kent State ROTC building, Governor Rhodes arrived in Kent to join the thousand or so National Guard troops deployed on campus and in town. At 10:00 a.m., Rhodes held a press conference in which, according to Phillip Caputo in his book *13 Seconds—A Look Back at the Kent State Shootings*, "He sounds like Joseph Conrad's Mister Kurtz in *Heart of Darkness*, scrawling in his diary his solution to the problem of rebellious natives in the Congo—*Exterminate the brutes.*"

The governor's remarks are directed toward outside agitators he holds responsible for the riots and damage of the prior two days. He describes the unidentified persons as "worse than brown shirts, worse than communists, the worse type of people we harbor in America," then concludes by promising to "eradicate the problem."

One theorist who believes a government conspiracy is at the heart of the Kent State Massacre is Alan Canfora, a victim wounded by National Guard bullets on May 4, 1970. On his Web site, www.alancanfora.com, Canfora opines the U.S. government conspired to commit a massacre at Kent State to terrorize the American student population into silencing the antiwar movement. Accordingly, he believes President Richard Nixon chose Kent State because of a long-standing friendship with Jim Rhodes and a grudge against Kent activists who had interrupted a speech at the University of Akron during the presidential campaign of 1968 and disrupted the inauguration parade in early 1969. For his part, Canora believes Rhodes participated because, in his term-limited final year as governor, he wanted to score votes from conservatives in the upcoming Ohio Republican U.S. Senate primary election.

"Personally, I blame the (Ohio National Guard) officers,

Governor Rhodes and President Nixon more than the lowly shooters who were just following orders, I think." So concludes Alan Canfora. James Rhodes lost the bid to become the Republican candidate from Ohio for the U.S. Senate; he lost by 1 percent of the vote. The election was held on May 5, 1970, one day after the Kent State Massacre.

CHARLES MANSON

Leaves Cincinnati, Gets in Trouble

9

Charlie Don't Surf
(On the Ohio)

Charles Manson

KATHLEEN MADDOX WAS A FUN-LOVING, rebellious teenager when she left what she felt to be an overly religious and strict family life in Ashland, Kentucky, in the early 1930s for big-city life in Cincinnati, Ohio. She liked to drink and reportedly kept company with a lot of young men. By November 12, 1934, sixteen-year-old Kathleen found herself at Cincinnati's General Hospital giving birth to a son, one Charles Milles Manson. Charles's surname came courtesy of one of Kathleen's boyfriends, namely twenty-four-year-old William Manson, a native of Cincinnati who listed his occupation as "laborer" in the "dry cleaning" business on Charles's birth certificate.

Although Kathleen Maddox and William Manson did marry for a brief time, William was never believed to be Charles's biological father. That distinction belonged to a man named Colonel Scott of Ashland, Kentucky. Kathleen sued Scott for paternity and child support in 1936, gaining a judgment against him that he ignored until his death in 1954. Colonel Scott never paid a cent toward support or acknowledged his son.

In 1939, Kathleen and her brother robbed a West Virginia gas station. For their efforts, each received a five-year prison term. Young Charlie was packed off to an aunt and uncle who reputedly bordered on religious fanaticism, giving young Manson the brunt to bear of his relative's disapproval of his heritage in general, and his mother's chosen lifestyle in particular.

By 1942 Kathleen was granted parole and regained custody of her now seven-year-old son. But she was certainly not reformed. Her heavy drinking and promiscuous lifestyle (some biographies say she was a prostitute) put Charlie second to his mother's vices. In 1947 Kathleen sought to rid herself of the responsibility of a son on the brink of becoming a teenager by shipping him off to the Gibault School for Boys in Terre Haute, Indiana.

Charlie ran away from the school after only a few months, returning to Cincinnati and his promiscuous, alcoholic mother. Kathleen Maddox still wanted nothing to do with her son, leaving him to a life on the streets, where survival meant committing thefts and other petit crimes. Charlie eventually made his way to Indiana, where he was arrested and placed in a juvenile detention facility. He escaped a day later. Upon recapture, Manson was sent to Father Flanagan's Boy's Town, where he lasted only five days before stealing a car and going on a robbery spree through Illinois. Busted again, Charlie drew a three-year sentence in a reform school at Plainfield, Indiana. It was here Manson claims to have been the victim of sexual assault at the hands of other inmates and guards alike. If you believe Charlie's account, Plainfield was a torture chamber where on one occasion a guard coerced other boys into assaulting and raping Manson while the officer watched and masturbated.

In February 1951, sixteen-year-old Charlie and two other inmates managed to escape from Plainfield. They immediately resumed stealing cars and headed west, garnering federal charges this time, when they were arrested in Beaver, Utah. Convicted of the federal crime of transporting stolen vehicles

"We're not in Wonderland

across state lines, Charlie was incarcerated in the minimum-security facility in the National Training School for Boys in Washington, D.C. That proved to be a bad move when in January 1952, Manson held a razor to another boy's throat and proceeded to sodomize him.

Reclassified as "dangerous" and promptly moved to a stricter lockup at the Federal Reformatory in Petersburg, Virginia, Charlie continued to be a disciplinary problem, accumulating eight major infractions, including three for homosexual assault. By August of 1952, his prison and probation reports read:

> Tries to give the impression of trying hard although actually not putting forth any effort ... marked degree of rejection, instability and psychic trauma ... constantly striving for status ... a fairly slick institutionalized youth who has not given up in terms of securing some kind of love and affection from the

world ... dangerous ... should not be trusted across the street ... homosexual and assaultive tendencies ... safe only under supervision ... unpredictable ... in spite of his age he is criminally sophisticated and grossly unsuited for retention in an open reformatory type institution.

Manson's record earned him a transfer to a more secure prison facility. He was sent back to his home state and the federal penitentiary at Chillicothe, Ohio. The Chillicothe "reformatory" indeed had an effect on Charlie as he became a "model prisoner." Most believe Charlie's "model" status was simply a ploy to get

anymore, Alice."

out of prison. If it was, it worked; he was paroled in May 1954.

After about six months of managing to avoid jail, Charlie married seventeen-year-old Rosalie Jean Willis in January 1955. By September of the same year, he was arrested again for an interstate road trip in a stolen vehicle. Rosalie Manson was pregnant at the time. Manson was sentenced to only five years' probation for the crime, but that was promptly revoked when he failed to appear in a Florida court to answer a separate stolen-vehicle charge. By March 1956, Charlie was again under arrest and on his way to Terminal Island, California. His son, Charles M. Manson, Jr., who committed suicide in 1993, was born around the same time. Rosalie divorced Manson, took up with a truck driver soon after, and she and Charles Jr. found their way out of Manson's life.

Charlie managed parole again in September 1958, after serving two years of a three-year sentence. By May 1959 he was back in jail in Los Angeles for forging and cashing stolen U.S. Treasury checks. Charlie's prison and probation reports were prophetic: "Almost without exception will let down anyone who went to bat for him ... an almost classic case of correctional institutional inmate ... a very difficult case and it is almost impossible to predict his future adjustment ... a very shaky probationer and it seems just a matter of time before he gets into further trouble."

Incredibly, Manson received probation again, which, again, was revoked in the spring of 1960, when he was charged with promoting prostitution and transporting women across state lines for the purpose of prostitution. Soon after his arrest, Charlie became a father for the second time. A girl he had met while managing to remain unincarcerated, "Leona," gave birth to Charles Luther Manson. Three people now shared Kathleen Maddox's father's first name.

This time around, Charlie was ordered to serve the ten-year sentence he received on the stolen check charges at McNeil Island Federal Penitentiary in Washington State. While at McNeil, Charlie met a member of the Depression-era criminal elite, Alvin "Creepy" Karpis, one of the leaders of the notorious Ma Barker gang, who had recently transferred from the soon-to-close Alcatraz. In his memoirs, *On The Rock: Twenty-Five Years at Alcatraz*, Karpis wrote of Manson:

> This kid approaches me to request music lessons. He wants to learn guitar and become a music star. "Little Charlie" is so lazy and shiftless, I doubt if he'll put [in] the time required to learn. The youngster has been in institutions all of his life—first orphanages, then reformatories, and finally federal prison. His mother, a prostitute, was never around to look after him. I decide it's time someone did something for him, and to my surprise, he learns quickly. He has a pleasant voice and a pleasing per-

Alvin "Creepy" Karpis

sonality, although he's unusually meek and mild for a convict. He never has a harsh word to say and is never involved in even an argument.

Manson knew Karpis had connections in Las Vegas and asked for a good word in helping to land a music gig there. Karpis declined, preferring to avoid the young con. Years later,

Karpis opined on the fate of his prison prodigy saying, "The history of crime in the United States might have been considerably altered if 'Little Charlie' had been given the opportunity to find fame and fortune in the music industry."

During his years in prison or on probation, Charlie had raped another inmate at razor point, stolen countless automobiles, pimped inmates, and forged stolen federal checks. His prison reports indicated no tendency toward rehabilitation while incarcerated, on probation, or into the future:

> He hides his resentment and hostility behind a mask of superficial ingratiation ... even his cries for help represent a desire for attention with only superficial meaning. Pattern of instability continues intense needs to call attention to himself ... fanatical interests. Manson is about to complete his ten year term. He has a pattern of criminal behavior and confinement that dates to his teen years ... little can be expected in the way of change.

Despite Charlie's own expressed desire to remain in jail, he was released in Los Angeles on March 21, 1967.

In the "Summer of Love," Charlie relocated to San Francisco's Haight-Ashbury district. The atmosphere of LSD, free love, and hundreds of disenfranchised kids appealed to Manson, who displayed a charisma some found mesmerizing. The "Manson Family" began to form from people hopelessly confused and often psychologically unbalanced who saw Charlie as a mentor, father figure, or even God. The "family" grew from thirty serious followers to an estimated fifty to a hundred members. They drifted around California from Haight-Ashbury to Hollywood, Los Angeles, and Death Valley associating with such unsavory groups as the Church of Satan, the Process Church of Final Judgment (another Satanist cult), and the Circle Order of the Dog Blood. All the while, Manson showed a growing obsession with death and his interpretation of "Helter Skelter," the Beatles song Charlie believed to be a prophetic prediction of an all-consuming race war in America. In his twisted view, Manson was convinced once "blackie" was incited to violence, the white race would be virtually annihilated, leaving Manson and his "family" royal sole rulers.

Manson believed "Helter Skelter" could be achieved by spectacular murder and mayhem to be blamed on blacks (although Manson himself claims the "racially motivated" murders were actually intended to confuse the evidence in another murder case). A number of grisly homicides committed toward this purpose have been specifically or generally attributed to the Manson Family between 1968 and the time the madness culminated on August 9, 1969.

Much has been written about the gruesome Tate and LaBianca murders committed by Manson Family members at Charlie's sick direction. "Helter Skelter" is described in books, journals, legal documents, news shows, and motion pictures. Photographs of the grisly crime scenes were widely distributed. In *Manson in His Own Words,* Charlie describes how members of the "family" decided to try to avert prosecution of one of their own who had been arrested for the bloody murder of drug dealer Gary Hinman in a transaction gone wrong. According to Manson, the Tate and LaBianca murders were, more or less, random acts designed to look "witchy" to trick authorities into believing there was a deranged serial killer at large, thereby proving family friend and incarcerated-at-the-time Hinman murder suspect Bobby Beausoleil was innocent and "like the same person that did Gary is still out there and doing it again."

Manson recalls being "totally without conscience" on the evening of August 8, 1969, when Susan Atkins emerged from the carload of fresh killers bragging, "Oh, Charlie, we did it! … I took

MURDERED!
Film star Sharon Tate

my life for you!" As Manson told author Nuel Emmons, he got a "complete run-down" of the terrible events from Charles "Tex" Watson and Susan "Sadie" Atkins. According to Manson, Tex drove to the home of music producer Terry Melcher in the wealthy neighborhood of Bel Air. He chose a house on a secluded lot and, as the women waited in the car, Watson climbed a telephone pole and cut the lines to the house. The four, Watson, Atkins, Patricia Krenwinkel, and Linda Kasabian climbed a fence and started up the drive toward the house. A car pulled up to the gate and stopped. Watson approached and summarily executed the teenage driver, Steven Parent, shooting him several times with a .22 pistol. At the house Watson broke in by cutting a screen, crawling through, and unlocking a rear door. He let Krenwinkel and Atkins in and stationed Kasabian as a lookout. What happened inside was a bloodbath that still haunts the American conscience. Voytek Frykowski, Jay Sebring, coffee heiress Abigail Folger and actress Sharon Tate and her unborn child were viciously slaughtered. According to Nuel Emmons, Manson claims he returned to the grisly scene to clean up any potential evidence left by his tribe of murderers.

The insanity didn't stop there. Not satisfied the Tate murders were enough to throw a red herring toward the Hinman killing, Manson decided on a sick encore performance. Charlie, Watson, Atkins, Krenwinkel, Kasabian, and newcomers Leslie Van Houten and Stephen "Clem" Grogan terrorized the home of Leno and Rosemary LaBianca, repeating the unimaginable on the couple at their address near Griffith Park. It was there one of the murderers misspelled "Healter Skelter" on the couple's refrigerator—using Rosemary LaBianca's blood.

One thing is certain, Cincinnati native Charlie Manson remains incarcerated for devising and orchestrating the Tate/LaBianca homicides. His criminal legacy now reaches legendary proportions.

Charles Manson at the Tate/LaBianca murder trial. Zealous follower Susan Atkins sits to his left.

WAYNE HAYS

Gives **Dictation** to Elizabeth **Ray**

10

The Congressman & the U.S. Secretary of Sex

IN 1949, OHIO'S 18TH CONGRESSIONAL District elected Wayne Hays to the United States House of Representatives to serve counties in the east-central part of the state. By the early 1970s, Representative Hays had risen to prominence in Washington as chairman of several committees, including the powerful House Administration Committee, which oversaw the physical plant needs of Capitol Hill. Not afraid to throw his weight around, he intimidated other lawmakers, who feared retaliation if they crossed him. He built a reputation for doing even small, spiteful things, such as having the air conditioning shut off in the office of an adversary.

Born May 13, 1911, in Belmont County, Wayne Levere Hays graduated from Ohio State University in 1933. He worked as a teacher in the Ohio towns of Flushing and Findlay throughout the 1930s. His political career began at the state level and progressed until he was elected to the 81st United States Congress, beginning service on January 3, 1949. He participated in the thirteen succeeding congresses.

Elizabeth Ray hit Capitol Hill in the early 1970s looking for a job and excitement. In her twenties by that time, Liz came from a deprived background in small-town North Carolina. Escaping marriage at an early age, Ray drifted from job to job and soon discovered her body to be a natural asset for getting what she wanted. She aspired to be an actress and spent time in New York and Hollywood. She became Miss Virginia 1975 during a stint on the beauty pageant circuit. Ray became intrigued with the idea of working in the most powerful political nerve center in the world. Upon arrival in D.C., she used her looks, sexual skills, and reputation to develop a network of liaisons with Washington's elite.

In her 1976 "novel," *The Washington Fringe Benefit*, Elizabeth Ray admitted, "In three years as a highly paid secretary for the United States government, despite my respectable cover, I was actually a political fringe benefit, and if my department were to have a name, it would have been called the Bureau of Erotic Affairs." By April 1974, Ray began working for Ohio's Congressman Hays as a clerk. Immediately after, as she later told the *Washington Post*, she was never asked to do any Congressional-related work and reported to her Capitol Hill office only once or twice a week for a couple hours at a time.

"Supposedly, I'm on the Oversight Committee," she told the *Post*, "but I call it the Out-of-Sight Committee."

Congressman Wayne Hays and family walk the White House lawn, while secretary Elizabeth Ray (inset) is nowhere to be seen.

By May 1976, Ray told reporters, Congressman Hays visited her once or twice a week for sex. At age sixty-four, Hays had divorced his wife of twenty-five years only months earlier, and in April married his longtime Ohio office secretary, Pat Peak, who continued to live in the Buckeye State. Close associates said Hays was planning on running as a favorite son presidential candidate in the June 8, 1976, Ohio primary, or trying for the governor's mansion in 1978. Elizabeth Ray says Congressman Hays assured her the party didn't have to end with his recent marriage. Liz told reporters she and the congressman had regular, if hurried, dinner dates, after which they adjourned to her Arlington, Virginia, apartment for sex. "He never stops in the living room," she said. "He walks right into the bedroom and he watches the digital clock. He's home by 9:30."

"Supposedly, I'm on the Oversight Committee,... but I call it the Out-of-Sight Committee."

Hays apparently grew nervous of the relationship at one point, suggesting to Ray she come into the office at least a couple hours a day. Apparently growing tired of the relationship with the abrasive congressman, Liz spouted her reason to *Washington Post* reporters for going public with the scandal: "I'm afraid of him. There are ten or fifteen offices [on the Hill] that I know girls have had to do this to get a job. Only mine is so cruel; the other congressmen at least treat them like a date. I used to go into depression, but I had to tell myself that it's a job I have to do right now."

Liz Ray's famous comment—"I can't type, I can't file, I can't even answer the phone"—received national attention and signaled the demise of "the meanest man in Congress."

Hays's response to the claim? "Hell's fire! I'm a very happily

SEX-RETARY!

Liz Ray can't type or answer the phone.

Elizabeth Ray capitalized on the scandal, publishing a book and appearing in Playboy magazine.

married man!"

But denial didn't work for Wayne Hays. He withdrew his name from the general election that year.

"I may never go down in history," Liz Ray later wrote, "but I am certainly going down *on it*."

"Sexual activity had become a routine part of the job which I accepted, because this was the nicest I'd ever had it, and I loved being up in the ivory tower of power."

Wayne Hays returned to Ohio, where he held office as a state senator briefly in 1979. He died in 1989 and was laid to rest in St. Clairsville. Elizabeth Ray tried to take advantage of her notoriety. She posed nude for *Playboy* and tried her hand at stand-up comedy. She has since faded into obscurity but managed to achieve a place in political scandal history.

LARRY
FLYNT

Rich Man,
Porn Man

11

The Hustler Obscenity Trial

Larry Flynt

EARLY 1977 FOUND THE CINCINNATI AREA gripped by the most frigid winter weather the city had seen in years. It was so cold the Ohio River froze, allowing pedestrians to cross back and forth between the Cincinnati and Covington shores on the ice *beneath* the Roebling Suspension Bridge. On the freezing Monday morning of January 24, however, things heated up a couple blocks uptown at the Hamilton County Courthouse. County Prosecutor Simon Leis, Jr., began opening statements in the trials of *Hustler* magazine publisher Larry Flynt, his wife

Althea, brother Jimmy, one of his managers, Al Van Schaik, and Flynt's Hustler Publishing Company. Flynt and the others faced misdemeanor charges of pandering obscenity by producing *Hustler* and the more serious felony charge of engaging in organized crime for conspiring with each other in the process (Ohio's organized crime statute makes it a felony in and of itself for five or more people to engage in a criminal enterprise).

Larry Flynt wasn't new to the greater Cincinnati area. A native of rural Kentucky, he eventually took up residence in Columbus, Ohio, and found success in a string of bars and nightclubs he opened across the state. By 1976, Flynt owned the Hustler Club in downtown Cincinnati near Sixth and Walnut streets. Two years earlier he had started *Hustler* magazine as a supplement to his growing sex-oriented entertainment businesses. Flynt had already found his way onto Simon Leis's radar screen before 1977 through a scandal involving a group of Cincinnati police officers that included then-Chief Carl Goodin in 1975. Although Flynt was never convicted of charges stemming from the incident, a grand jury accused him of providing women for "sex parties" with the police.

Simon Leis, Jr., became Hamilton County Prosecutor in 1971. An ex-Marine officer, Leis's reputation as a champion of morality was sealed in 1975 when he successfully prosecuted Chief Goodin on indictments alleging "kickbacks" and corruption in the police department (Goodin's conviction was later overturned on appeal).

Leis opened the Flynt trial contending Flynt and the co-defendants conspired with a Cincinnati magazine distributor, Marshall News Co., to distribute eleven monthly issues of *Hustler* in Hamilton County between July 1975 and May 1976. They contended the magazines contained "lustful photographs and articles ranging from bestiality, sadism and bondage to 'threesome' sex and sex orgies." Flynt's attorney, Harold

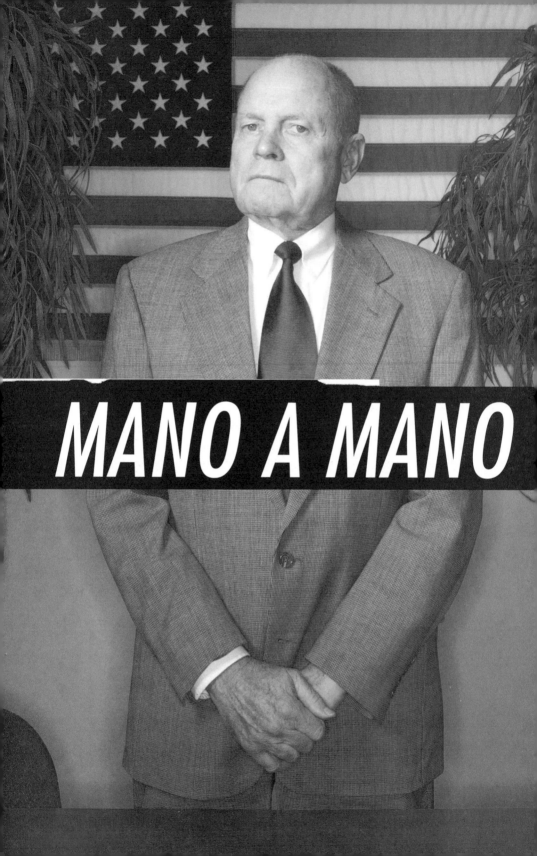

Larry Flynt faced Hamilton County Prosecutor Simon Leis (opposite) in the battle over Hustler.

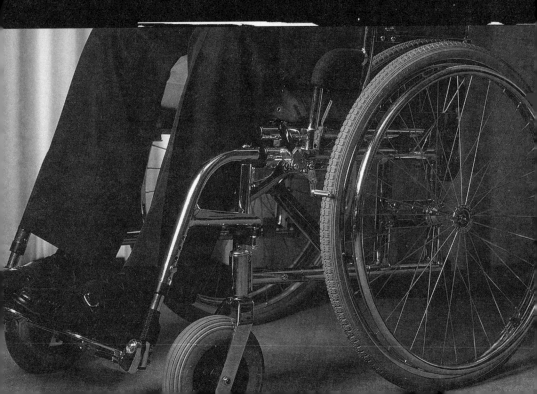

Fahringer, had experience defending obscenity cases. Traveling from Buffalo, New York, for the trial, Fahringer told jurors, "Obscenity is in the eye of the beholder." To support his point, he noted the fact that five other "girlie" magazines, along with *Hustler*, sold 925,000 copies in Hamilton County in the eleven months covered in the indictment, adding that this was "pretty compelling proof of community standards."

Defendant Flynt had little faith in the jurors at his trial as he mentions in his 1996 autobiography, *An Unseemly Man*:

> The problem with selecting jurors for my obscenity trial was primarily the difficulty of finding objective and non-repressed people. Jurors who were repressed, impotent, frigid or otherwise sexually frustrated would vote "guilty" for sure. If they didn't they would have to admit that they had spent all their lives missing out on one of the best things life had to offer. How many people would admit to that? And how many sexually open people could there be in a city that was so frightened by sex?

Fueling Flynt's concern was the 1973 Supreme Court decision in the case Miller vs. California, which left the issue of determining what is or is not obscene to community standards. This decision meant the members of the jury were solely responsible for determining if the contents of *Hustler* qualified as pornography. The decision on obscenity belonged to the jurors. If the defendants were guilty of pandering obscenity, for his part, Leis needed only to convince the jury the defendants and *Hustler* had worked together to publish and distribute the magazine in Hamilton County. Of course this didn't stop the prosecutor from seizing every opportunity to describe to the jurors bits and pieces of *Hustler* material, including a cartoon of Santa Claus in a compromising situation and a life-size blowup photo of Althea's nude centerfold appearance.

Each side presented its own "expert" witnesses to try to define "pornography." The prosecution even called a local television station news anchor, Al Schottelkotte, as a rebuttal witness to give the results of a "random" telephone poll TV station WCPO had taken of Hamilton County residents asking if they found *Hustler* obscene. Schottelkotte told the jury that, according to the poll, of the 470 respondents, 47 percent said magazines depicting sexual acts and nudity should be declared legally obscene, 29.4 percent said no, and 23.6 percent were undecided. The defense quickly countered by getting Schottelkotte to admit the poll was, to say the least, administered "unscientifically."

Closing arguments began on February 2, when First

"Obscenity is in the eye of the beholder."

Assistant Prosecutor Fred Cartolano, who later became a common pleas judge, told the jury, "I have a disadvantage talking to you here because you haven't seen the magazines. When you get the magazines, if you're like most people, it's going to blow your minds. They're the nightmare of a degenerate."

"It baffles me," countered Harold Fahringer. "We agree we have a right to read what we want, but this is meaningless if you can't go out and buy it. Freedom is what this is all about—freedom of the press." Simon Leis concluded closing arguments by telling the jury, "It's time to draw the line on obscenity," as he metaphorically used a piece of chalk to draw a line across the courtroom floor.

Judge William Morrissey gave the jury its instructions and sent it to deliberations the afternoon of February 3. After four days and a weekend off, the jury announced its verdict to a packed courtroom on Tuesday, February 8, 1977.

"Guilty!" came the verdict for Larry, "on all counts." Jimmy Flynt, Althea Leasure Flynt, and Al Van Schaik were all acquitted, but the court erupted around key defendant Larry Flynt as he was unceremoniously handcuffed and taken before the judge for an unusual immediate sentencing.

"You haven't made an intelligent decision through the course of this trial," Flynt told Morrissey. "I don't expect one now!" The judge responded on the spot, pronouncing a sentence of seven to twenty-five years in prison and $11,000 in fines. Bond denied, Flynt was led off to jail, but not before Judge Morrissey made public the news of more indictments against Larry Flynt for depicting gruesome war casualties in 400,000 pamphlets that were mailed to Hamilton County residents a month before the trial in December 1976.

Flynt's actual jail time lasted a little over a week. His conviction in the Cincinnati trial was eventually overturned by the Ohio Supreme Court. Flynt runs Hustler Publishing to this day. Leis is now sheriff of Hamilton County. Jimmy Flynt runs Hustler Hollywood stores in downtown Cincinnati and Butler County, Ohio.

More than thirty years later, Larry Flynt remains visible in Hamilton County with his store in downtown Cincinnati run by brother Jimmy.

GERALD ROBINSON

Father Murders Sister

12

Bizarre Murder among the Clergy in Toledo

SPRING HADN'T QUITE ARRIVED ON THE COLD, early-April Easter weekend of 1980 at Mercy Hospital on the edge of downtown Toledo. The hospital was operated by the Roman Catholic order Sisters of Mercy, and the seventeen resident nuns prepared for Holy Saturday services to be held in the hospital chapel on the afternoon of April 5. Sister Madeline Marie, the chapel organist, checked her instrument for the usual list of hymns she was to perform at the Mass. Unable to locate the list, the nun went to the sacristy, a small preparation room off the chapel, to use the telephone to call the priest who would make the decision on music for the service. Inside the sacristy she saw what she believed at first to be a CPR dummy lying on the terrazzo floor. Thinking it unusual, Sister Madeline took a closer look. What she saw caused a shriek to rival the musical notes she intended to play.

The organist discovered the brutally abused body of seventy-two-year-old Sister Margaret Ann Pahl. Sister Pahl had been strangled, stabbed repeatedly, and sexually defiled. She was dead by the time doctors reached her. Toledo police had a bizarre murder on their hands, so bizarre, in fact, it defied the senses. So crazy, it would take twenty-six years to solve, and jar the very foundations of the Roman Catholic Church in the Diocese of Toledo.

During the original investigation of Sister Margaret Pahl's murder, it soon became clear the one viable suspect was, incredible to many, a Catholic priest named Father Gerald Robinson. In the tight-knit Polish Catholic community of Toledo, the faithful were accustomed to holding clergy in reverence. It would take powerful persuasion to convince some that "Father Jerry," or any priest for that matter, was capable of such a sick and despicable crime. This may have been the case with then-Toledo Deputy Police Chief Ray Vetter, who investigators say put an effective halt to the investigation when he interrupted, and eventually put an end to, interrogations of Father Robinson despite the compelling evidence against him.

Whatever the reason, Sister Margaret Ann Pahl's murder soon took on "cold case" status due to "lack of evidence." She was buried on April 8, 1980, in St. Bernadine Cemetery on the grounds of Our Lady of the Pines Retreat Center in Fremont, Ohio. Evidence in the case, including a sword-shaped letter opener owned by Gerald Robinson, found its way into storage, where it would sit waiting for twenty-three years.

Fast forward to 2002. A child-abuse scandal hits the

Catholic church from coast to coast. In Toledo, horrible memories creep back into the psyche of a Roman Catholic nun who remembers being victimized by a satanic cult while she was a student in a Toledo parochial school. The sister's charges include graphic descriptions of rape, bloody violence, even the murder of other children at the hands of a satanic cult seemingly headed, she says, by Father Chet Warren, an oblate of the order of St. Francis de Sales. Of the many atrocities perpetrated against her, one in particular puts the name Father Gerald Robinson back on the police radar screen.

The now forty-something-year-old nun claims, during the height of her terrible ordeal, Father Chet Warren played pimp, using her as a child prostitute. While Warren was chaplain at Toledo's St. Vincent Hospital, the nun said, her father, also a cult member, would drive the high school girl to the hospital and turn her over to Warren, who in turn would take her to his apartment, where men would pay him to have sadomasochist sex with her. One of the "customers" she identified by name was Father Gerald Robinson.

After telling her story under assurance of anonymity, she was met with disbelief. Her tale was categorically dismissed as "not credible" by the Toledo Diocese Review Board assembled to investigate such claims. Like many victims of the "clergy abuse crisis" in the Catholic Church, resolution would not come easy for the nun. But two detectives on the relatively new Lucas County Prosecutor's cold-case squad took note of one aspect of the story. They recognized the name of Father Gerald Robinson, former chaplain in residence at Mercy Hospital and the sole suspect in what appeared to be the bizarre ritual-style murder of Sister Margaret Ann Pahl.

Steve Forrester and Tom Ross were both veteran investigators by the time they looked into Sister Pahl's twenty-three-year-old murder in 2003. But what they found as they sorted through

Father Gerald Robinson, 1968

the boxes of evidence was new to both. With the help of Dr. Dawn Perlmutter, the director of the Institute for the Research of Organized and Ritual Violence, the detectives determined the 1980 murder of Sister Margaret Ann Pahl was in fact "about as classic as it gets" for a satanic ritual murder. Dr.

173

Sister Margaret Ann Pahl

Perlmutter detailed the reasons for her conclusion in a lengthy report to the Lucas County prosecutor's office.

First she pointed out the location of the murder strongly suggested satanic ritual. "The murder was committed in a sacred place, in the sacristy of a chapel," she said in the report. "In satanic crimes, perpetrators choose Christian sacred places because it literally and symbolically increases the desecration of Christianity and ritually enhances magical powers."

Another indication of satanic ritual was the timing of the sister's murder, the doctor contended. "The murder occurred on April 5, 1980, Holy Saturday. Easter is the most important holiday of the Christian year and committing the murder on Easter intensifies the desecration."

The third sign, according to Dr. Perlmutter, was Sister Margaret Ann's character. "From a traditional satanic perspective, Sister Margaret Ann Pahl was an ideal victim. In ritual killings of both animals and humans, the sacrificial offering is chosen because of its attributes. For example, historically it would be ineffective to sacrifice a sick or wounded animal; it has to be the finest specimen so that the gods are not offended. In satanism, the ideal victim is someone who represents a virtuous life dedicated to serving God. Sacrificing a nun would be considered a powerful accomplishment for the perpetrator."

She continued: "In satanism, it is very important to mock the Christian religion. The significance is to desecrate the objects, which will evoke a stronger magical experience."

Use of the victim's blood, a stab pattern in the form of an upside-down cross, the sexual defilement, and the identification of Father Robinson's pentagram-inscribed sword-shaped letter opener as the murder weapon were all indicators of a satanic ritual, according to Dr. Perlmutter. A strange case was getting stranger.

Forrester and Ross had forensic tools not available to

Father Gerald Robinson surrounded by his defense team at his trial in 2006.

investigators in 1980. They pursued potential leads through the use of modern DNA methods, even up to exhumation and reexamination of Sister Margaret Ann's body. The detectives also used contemporary techniques such as "blood spatter" evidence seeking out the help of up-and-coming experts in the field like Dr. Henry Lee, the forensics expert who found international prominence after testifying in the O.J. Simpson trial. Forrester and Ross even located key witnesses whose stories had been ignored, overlooked, or never sought twenty-three years earlier. Detective Forrester even received a search warrant for the "secret records" of the Diocese of Toledo after it was discovered the diocese's chancellor and bishop may have been withholding information in conformity with a little-known section of Roman Catholic Canon Law that required

"... She was strangled to the very

the diocese's hierarchy not only to maintain such records but to also generally deny their existence. The detectives seized 145 additional pages in the search.

As the investigation continued, the circumstantial case against Father Robinson grew until April 23, 2004, when the veteran Catholic priest was arrested and formally charged with the murder of Sister Margaret Ann Pahl. The stage was set for a trial, twenty-three years late in coming that was garnering national and international attention.

The finale opened on April 26, 2006, officially twenty-six years after the bloody Easter weekend in the chapel sacristy at Mercy Hospital. That day, for the first time as far as anyone could tell, a Catholic priest went on trial for the murder of a Catholic nun. Lucas County Assistant Prosecutor Dean

Mandros made an opening statement describing the horrible fate of Sister Margaret Ann Pahl: "It was in the sacristy of that chapel that someone took her by the neck and choked her. The killer choked her so hard that two bones inside her neck broke. He choked her so hard that the blood vessels inside her eyes burst. She was strangled to the very verge of death, but not quite."

"The killer laid her upon the floor," Mandros continued, "after laying her on the floor, he covered her with a white altar cloth. After doing that, he stabbed her over the heart nine times. Nine piercings of her flesh in the shape of an upside-down cross.

"And after he did all that, he does some more. He takes off the altar cloth, he stabs her twenty-two more times. This time he's still not through. After doing these things, he pulls up her

verge of death, but not quite."

dress, her smock, up over her chest. He pulls her girdle, her underpants, her hose, down to her ankles. He leaves her exposed, naked, stretched out like in a coffin, on the sacristy floor. Only then is the killer done."

The trial and deliberations concluded the morning of May 11, 2006. Father Gerald Robinson, a priest in the Diocese of Toledo for over forty years, was found guilty by a jury of his peers in the brutal 1980 slaying of fellow clergy member Sister Margaret Ann Pahl. He was immediately handcuffed and led off to a jail cell. He is currently residing in a facility provided by the Ohio Department of Corrections and Rehabilitation. Depending on the outcome of expected appeals, Gerald Robinson will be eligible for parole in 2021.

SAM SHEPPARD

Murder on Suburbia's Beach

13

Dr. Sam Goes Down for the Count

Dr. Sam Sheppard

ON APRIL 6, 1970, FORTY-SIX-YEAR-OLD professional wrestler Sam Sheppard, known as "Doctor" because of the signature "nerve hold" he allegedly developed as a neurologist, was found dead in his Columbus apartment. Known to drink as much as two fifths of liquor a day, the wrestler's cause of death was listed as liver failure.

Marilyn and Sam Sheppard's wedding photo

Sam Sheppard never planned on joining the wrestling circuit. Just sixteen years earlier, in 1954, he was living an idyllic life with his wife, Marilyn, and their seven-year-old son, Sam, also called "Chip," in the quiet Cleveland suburb of Bay Village on the Lake Erie shore. At that time he really was a doctor—Dr. Samuel Holmes Sheppard, known to many people as "Doctor Sam," a well-respected physician who helped run Bay View Hospital, a 110-bed osteopathic institution converted from an eighty-year-old mansion. Through his work Dr. Sam

183

earned a good living, affording him a lakefront home and a Lincoln Continental and Jaguar in the garage. Sheppard's life took the first in what would be a series of dark turns in 1954 early one Sunday morning on a hot Fourth of July weekend.

Sam Sheppard repeated the horrific story of what he says happened that night dozens of times over the following two decades. As he tells it, he and Marilyn bid goodnight to dinner guests, neighbors Don and Nancy Ahern, around midnight, and Sam settled in to watch the late movie, *Strange Holiday*, on the living room couch while Marilyn went to sleep in the couple's upstairs bedroom. Sam said he fell asleep watching television and was startled awake some time later, believing his wife was calling his name.

He says he ran upstairs seeing, "a form of light garment, I believe, at the same time grappling with something or someone." Sheppard says he heard moans and groans when he was suddenly struck from behind and lost consciousness. When he came to, Sam said he was lying on the floor. He noticed Marilyn covered in blood. He checked her pulse and realized she was dead. He ran to the next room, where he found Chip undisturbed and still sleeping soundly.

Alerted by a noise downstairs, Sam says he ran to the back door, which he found open, when he noticed "a form progressing rapidly toward the lake." He says the figure was about six foot three, middle aged, with dark bushy hair and a white shirt. Sheppard says he chased the man across the lawn and down the wooden steps to the lakefront beach fifty feet below. Then, he said, "I lunged or jumped and grasped him in some manner from the back, either body or leg." The two struggled until, as Sam put it, he felt himself "twisting or choking, and this terminated my consciousness."

Sam said he had no idea how long he was out. When he came to, he made his way back to his wife in the upstairs bedroom. "I believed or thought I was disoriented, and the victim of a bizarre dream, and I believe I paced in and out of the room and possibly into other rooms. I may have reexamined her, finally believing that this was true."

Stunned and confused, Sheppard said he vaguely remembers calling his neighbor and friend Bay Village Mayor Spencer Houk. Houk said Dr. Sam told him, "For God's sake, Spen, get over here. I think they've killed Marilyn." As dawn broke over Bay Village, Mayor Houk and his wife, Esther, entered the blood-spattered bedroom of the Sheppard home. Marilyn's body was barely recognizable. Houk phoned the police.

Around 6:02 a.m. Bay Village Police Officer Fred Drenkhan arrived. Drenkhan knew Dr. Sam well because Sheppard served as police surgeon in the community and often rode on police patrols. When Drenkhan saw Marilyn's body and the carnage, he suggested to Mayor Houk that an ensuing investigation would be better served by an agency with more resources. Houk agreed and called on the Cleveland Police Department, which immediately dispatched a specialist from the Scientific Investigation Unit along with a veteran team of homicide detectives, Robert Schottke and Patrick Gareau.

In the meantime Dr. Sam's brother, Dr. Steve, had arrived and taken Sam to Bay Village Hospital, where he was admitted with his injuries. Sheppard's other brother, Dr. Richard, also arrived and took Chip back to his home. The news had traveled fast, and soon the crime scene and surrounding neighborhood was crowded with police cars, reporters, curiosity seekers, and friends of the Sheppards. As neighborhood boys lingered in the Sheppard's yard, sixteen-year-old Larry Houk, the mayor's son, noticed Dr. Sam's medical bag lying in the weeds on the hillside leading to the waterfront. Inside the case were Dr. Sam's wristwatch, fraternity ring from Hanover College, and his keys. The bag, like several other items at the scene, were all handled by

185

several people before forensic checks could be conducted by investigators. At the crime scene, it appeared that no one was clear on who was in charge of the investigation. When veteran Cuyahoga County Coroner Samuel R. Gerber arrived at 8 a.m., reporters flocked to him for answers.

Dr. Gerber, who was also involved in Cleveland's notorious "Kingsbury Run Butcher" murders, had held the coroner's post in Cuyahoga County for eighteen years before taking on the Sheppard case. Reporters counted on Gerber for the kind of information they needed to sensationalize a story. He didn't disappoint them with the Bay Village murder. "He rained blow after blow on her with savage fury," Gerber told the press while describing the wounds to Mrs. Sheppard's head. He also said there appeared to be no evidence of a break-in.

By the time Cleveland detectives Schottke and Gareau made it to the hospital to interview Dr. Sam—who was reportedly suffering from bruises, chipped teeth, and a fractured vertebra in his neck—he had been sedated. The investigators also learned that Dr. Gerber had arrived at the hospital earlier, interviewing Sheppard and collecting the clothing he was wearing when admitted. They returned to the crime scene to question neighbors. Gerber had already returned to the Sheppard residence, where he was holding court with reporters.

When the homicide detectives returned to interview Dr. Sam again, they were armed with some tough questions. Was his relationship with Marilyn troubled? What was his involvement with a former Bay View nurse named Susan Hayes? How did he account for being knocked out, not once but twice, by a "mysterious form"? What happened in the two or three hours between Marilyn's murder and the time he called Mayor Houk? Why wasn't there any evidence of forced entry into the house? Why couldn't police locate fingerprints in the house? How had their son slept through the brutal murder and subsequent scuffles

Sheppard had with the "bushy-haired man"? Why had the Sheppard's dog never stirred? Where was the T-shirt Dr. Sam had been wearing when the Aherns left the house around midnight?

Time after time, Sam Sheppard replied, "I don't know." At the end of the interview, Detective Schottke told Sam, "I think you killed your wife." Schottke also recommended Sheppard's arrest for the crime to Mayor Houk and Bay Village Police Chief John Eaton, but they were hesitant. The story remained front-page news.

Marilyn Sheppard's funeral was held on July 5. Sam attended in a wheelchair and wearing an orthopedic collar. He wept during the eulogy. Investigators began to object to the claim by Sheppard's doctor, his brother Steve, that the patient was in no condition to answer questions.

"We expected cooperation from the family, but we don't seem to be getting it," Coroner Gerber told the press. "Here's a witness surrounded by his whole family of doctors." Assistant Cuyahoga County Prosecutor John Mahon added, "In my twenty-three years of criminal prosecution, I have never seen such flagrant stalling."

Apparently concerned about the publicity, Dr. Sam announced a $10,000 reward for information leading to the capture of the murderer, asserting, "I have never refused to talk to any authorities or give them any information I had." By Thursday Dr. Sheppard agreed to accompany the police back to his house for a tour of the scene. When he arrived, he was shocked to see a crowd of onlookers, photographers, and reporters on his lawn. The media were even permitted to attend and photograph the event. Although news coverage originally appeared sympathetic to young Dr. Sam, the *Cleveland Press*'s coverage of the event hinted at a shift in sentiment. "Flanked by two lawyers," they wrote, "Dr. Samuel H. Sheppard today re-enacted his version of the murder of his pretty wife Marilyn—and repeated it, detail by detail, word for word, over and over again."

Cleveland police continued to encourage Bay Village to arrest Samuel Sheppard. Ohio law at the time allowed a "reasonable period" of detention for suspects of serious felonies allowing authorities the opportunity for intensive interrogation during which the suspect would likely "break down." Bay Village continued to hesitate, and the *Press* took note in a July 16 editorial titled "The Finger of Suspicion." The newspaper complained the case was hindered by "the hostility of Bay Village officials to any 'outsiders' in this case" and "the unusual protection set up around the husband of the victim, the sole witness. Every further moment of fumbling is helping a murderer escape." Less than a week later, on July 21, the *Press* followed up with another editorial, this time on the front page, entitled "Why No Inquest? Do It Now, Dr. Gerber." By that afternoon, the coroner's office announced an inquest.

Bay Village hosted the inquest in the auditorium of Normandy Elementary School. Coroner Gerber presided and, noting it was not a court proceeding, ruled that Dr. Sheppard's lawyer, William Corrigan, could not participate. Although Sam Sheppard was now clearly a suspect, and was constitutionally protected from testifying at the inquest, he answered Gerber's questions promptly.

When the questions came to the stability of the marriage and rumors of adulterous indiscretions, Sam told the inquest he had not discussed divorce with his wife "in a serious fashion," and as far as Susan Hayes was concerned, although he had seen her on a recent trip to Los Angeles, he had never had sex with her. He also admitted he had not slept in the same bedroom with Marilyn for four nights in a row prior to her murder. A chill seemed to come over the spectators.

On the last day of the inquest, attorney Corrigan tried to get some comments favorable to his client on record. The *Cleveland*

Plain Dealer described the result in an article entitled "Corrigan Ejected Amid Cheers": "Spectators cheered wildly as William J. Corrigan, criminal lawyer representing Dr. Samuel H. Sheppard, was half-dragged from the room in the closing moments of the Marilyn Sheppard inquest in Bay Village."

By the next afternoon, the media feeding frenzy took another bite out of Dr. Sam when the headlines exclaimed, "Susan Hayes Admits Affair, Flies to City." The article was accompanied by a photo of prosecutor Mahon and Detective Schottke boarding a plane with Ms. Hayes at the Los Angeles Airport. Stories and pictures of "brown-eyed Susan Hayes" dominated Cleveland front pages, culminating with comments to a *Press* reporter: "Doctor Lies, Susan Charges; Tells of Gifts, Marriage Talk." The article went on to describe Hayes's account of an affair with Dr. Sam that included earlier sexual encounters in his car, his office above the Sheppard Clinic in nearby Fairview Park, and at her Los Angeles apartment earlier in 1954.

The media attention proved to be more than local officials could tolerate, and on July 29, twenty-five days after Marilyn's murder, Cuyahoga County Prosecutor Frank Cullitan gave Bay Village authorities an ultimatum: Sheppard had to be arrested or Cleveland police were pulling out of the case.

The pressure took its toll on the Bay Village officials. Its law director, Richard Weygandt, took the facts "under review." Part-time Mayor Houk, whose full-time occupation was running a meat market across from City Hall, had to be put to bed under sedation. The next day the *Press* ran an eight-column editorial demanding that Bay Village "quit stalling and bring him in!" Dr. Sam was promptly arrested with much media attention and fanfare. His only comment to the multitude of reporters and television cameras on the scene: "Apparently the press had its way."

At 9 a.m. on October 18, 1954, the Court of Common Pleas for Cuyahoga County was called to order in the courtroom of

Judge Edward J. Blythin in the case of the State of Ohio vs. Samuel H. Sheppard. The courtroom was crammed with local and national media. Despite defense counsel Corrigan's motion for a change of venue, a jury was seated and the trial began November 4.

The first witness, Deputy Coroner Lester Adelson, described the autopsy performed on Marilyn Sheppard's body showing gruesome photos of the bloody crime scene and the victim's battered face. Sam could not look at them. During cross-examination Corrigan got Adelson to admit he made no analysis of the contents of the victim's stomach, did not make microscopic study of her wounds, and did not determine if she had been sexually assaulted.

The Aherns followed, with Mrs. Ahern saying Marilyn had confided in her about marital difficulties, including a riff about Sam's purchase of a watch for Susan Hayes. Other key players gave their accounts to the jury. Susan Hayes took the stand and admitted to a prolonged sexual relationship with Dr. Sam.

The defense was equally as tenacious in its contention that there was never a problem in the Sheppard marriage. Sam himself testified about the two-year affair between him and Susan Hayes. He vehemently denied killing his wife. In its summation, the prosecution tried to appeal to the jury's logic: "If the burglar was in that room and took the time and trouble to strike all those vicious blows on Marilyn, I ask you why the assailant did not use that same instrument, not to hit Sam thirty-five times, but to strike one single blow against him. A burglar does not want to leave a living witness at the scene of a crime." The prosecutor added: "Be fair to the defendant. Show him the same mercy he showed his victim."

Defense attorney Corrigan countered: "The fact that Sam Sheppard strayed is no proof that he did not love his wife, his child, and his home." He took note of the "trial by newspaper," telling jurors: "If you read a story like this about the People's Court in China or behind the Iron Curtain, it would raise your hair on your head. But this is something that happened in our own city of Cleveland!" The judge read his charge to the jury. After six weeks of testimony, Sam Sheppard's fate rested with them.

After one hundred hours of deliberation, the jury reached a verdict. They found Dr. Sam not guilty of murder in the first degree but guilty of second-degree murder. When Judge Edward Blythin asked the defendant if he had anything to say, Sheppard replied, "I would like to say, sir, that I am not guilty, and I feel there have been facts presented before this court that definitely have proven that I couldn't have performed this crime." Over defense objections, the judge passed immediate sentence—life in prison. Weeks later, the dying continued when Sam Sheppard's mother was found with a bullet in her brain. "I just can't go on," she wrote in a letter to Sam's brother, Steve. "Thanks for everything." Eleven days later, Sheppard's father died of a hemorrhaging gastric ulcer. The family was convinced it was caused by the stress of their recent troubles.

Appeals filed on behalf of Sam Sheppard were many, but largely unfruitful until William Corrigan died in 1961, and the Sheppard family enlisted the help of a young hotshot lawyer named F. Lee Bailey. In April 1963, Bailey filed a writ of habeas corpus in federal court charging Sheppard's constitutional right to a fair trial had been denied in the media circus surrounding the proceedings and the trial judge's failure to grant a change of venue and/or protect jurors from the ample prejudicial pretrial publicity. And, while it wouldn't help in a court of law, the court of public opinion was swaying in favor of Sam Sheppard.

A number of books and magazine articles supporting Sheppard's cause had been published since the conviction, and a popular television drama series, *The Fugitive*, allowed audi-

"I would like to say, sir, that I am not guilty . . ."

(far left) Dr. Sam is led from the courtroom after sentencing, a photo of his son clutched in his hand. (left) Dr. Sam with new wife Ariane and son Chip not long after his release. (above) Defense attorney F. Lee Bailey, Dr. Sam, Ariane.

ences to follow the adventures of Dr. Richard Kimble, played by actor David Janssen, as he tried to prove his innocence in the murder of his wife at the hands of the "one-armed man." Though the show's creator denied any creative connection to the Sheppard case, it was assumed at the time—and the similarities make it difficult even today to believe Dr. Sam's widely publicized situation didn't exert some influence in the show's development—that the show was based on the Cleveland murder case. The popularity of *The Fugitive* certainly didn't hurt the growing sense of sympathy for the doctor.

On July 16, 1964, over ten years after the murder, Federal District Judge Carl Weinman of Dayton ordered that Sam Sheppard be released from prison, stating, "If there ever was a trial by newspaper, this is a perfect example. And the most insidious violator was the *Cleveland Press*." Weinman cited five separate violations of Sheppard's constitutional rights, noting, "Each of the ... errors is by itself sufficient to require a determination that petitioner was not afforded a fair trial as required by the due process clause of the Fourteenth Amendment. And when errors are cumulated, the trial can only be viewed as a mockery of justice."

Sam Sheppard was out of jail. Moreover, his case and incarceration had attracted a devoted fan. Ariane Tebbenjohans, a thirty-three-year-old buxom blond divorcée from Germany had corresponded with Sam since she read of his plight in a German magazine. In 1963 Ariane visited Sam in the Ohio State Penitentiary in Columbus. Shortly after his release, the two were married. Pictures of the happy doctor with his glamorous new wife appeared in the media, tempering the public's sympathy a bit for Sheppard.

The courts were not yet finished with Sam Sheppard. In May of 1965 a federal appeals court ruled to reinstate the conviction. The U.S. Supreme Court agreed to hear the case, and Sam remained free, albeit in legal limbo.

The Supreme Court ruled in 1966 that Sam Sheppard, after twelve years—ten of which were spent in prison—was legally an innocent man. "The massive, pervasive and prejudicial publicity attending the petitioner's prosecution prevented him from receiving a fair trial consistent with the Due Process Clause of the Fourteenth Amendment," wrote Justice Tom Clark. "Despite his awareness of the excessive pretrial publicity, the judge failed to take effective measures against the massive publicity which continued throughout the trial or to take adequate steps to control the conduct of the trial." Free at last—until a new trial could be arranged.

Sam Sheppard had another day in court on November 1, 1966—sixteen days shy of twelve years since the first trial. This time jurors acquitted him on the grounds that they thought the police investigation was sloppy, and they saw a lack of motive. Things were looking up for Samuel Holmes Sheppard. Or were they?

Sheppard's last attorney, F. Lee Bailey, wrote in his book *The Defense Never Rests* of Sam Sheppard's quick trip down the slippery slope of alcohol and drugs shortly after his release from prison. Readmitted to the practice of medicine, he was sued for malpractice in the death of a patient. Ariane filed for divorce in 1968, saying that Dr. Sam, while under the influence of drugs and booze, had stolen from her and threatened her with violence. In 1969, after he had moved to Columbus and become a professional wrestler, he allegedly married Colleen Strickland, his wrestling manager's twenty-year-old daughter, while on a motorcycle trip to Mexico. Sheppard died on that early spring day in 1970 drunk and financially insolvent.

In 1995, his son Chip coauthored a book in which he put it more succinctly: "Medical terms don't fully capture what killed Dr. Sam. He really died of a broken heart and a spirit that found no solace."

OHIO
POLITICAL
PECCADILLOES

14

POLITICAL SCANDAL AND CORRUPTION SEEM
to be as American as red, white, and blue, and
Ohio politicos have certainly done their part to
contribute to the reputation. Even before the
Buckeye State became a state, our founding
fathers pioneered ways to create the stuff gossip, criminal indictments, and legends are made
of. Some are even surprised that Governor Bob
Taft waited until the new millennium to become the
first sitting Ohio chief executive to be convicted of
a crime (nobody golfs for free!). One thing's for
sure: The stories in this chapter won't be the last to
grace the annals of Ohio history.

The 100 Year Presidential Curse

Before becoming a U.S. representative and senator from Ohio, and eventually the ninth president of the United States, **William Henry Harrison** found fame as an Indian fighter. Defeating a loosely knit group of tribes led by the Shawnee chief Tecumseh at the Battle of Tippecanoe earned Harrison the nickname "Old Tippecanoe." Harrison's victories over the Indians allowed settlers to expand through vast portions of what are now Ohio and Indiana. The conflicts culminated in 1809 after Harrison secured 2.5 million acres of Indian land after the Treaty of Ft. Wayne.

Two Native American leaders of the Shawnee tribe, Tecumseh and Tenskwatawa ("The Prophet") resisted what they saw as encroachment of their land. They organized a confederation of like-minded Native Americans of various tribes to fight settlers' westward expansion. In 1811, Harrison, then territorial governor, received authorization to assume command of an army to march against any Indian uprising. He earned his nickname after victory at the fierce battle at Prophetstown, next to the Wabash and Tippecanoe rivers.

The defeat foiled Tecumseh's plan to organize resistance, and he became increasingly bitter toward Harrison. For his part, Old Tippecanoe saw the defeat of the Shawnee as a political feather in his cap to serve as a stepping stone to higher office. Tecumseh sided with the British in the War of 1812, and he died at the Battle of the Thames at the hands of American soldiers who were once again commanded by Harrison. According to Joel Martin and William J. Birnes, authors of *The Haunting of the Presidents*, Tenskwatawa, Tecumseh's younger brother, grew to despise Harrison and all he stood for.

OLD TIPPECANOE!
President William Henry Harrison

Tenskwatawa was known among the Shawnee as a prophet and a holy man with remarkable paranormal abilities. He deeply resented the white man's westward movement and instructed his followers to avoid settlers, whom he described as "children of the Evil Spirit." To William Henry Harrison, the Prophet was an "imposter," about whom he said, according to Martin and Birnes, "If he really is a prophet, ask him to cause the sun to stand still, the moon to alter its course, the rivers to cease to flow, or the dead to rise from their graves. If he does these things, you may believe he has been sent from God."

Tenskwatawa answered the challenge when, remarkably, he predicted a solar eclipse that partially covered the sun. He also forewarned of an earthquake that struck the Midwest on December 16, 1811. The event was of such magnitude "the Mississippi and Ohio Rivers flowed backwards." Followers and enemies alike began to take Tenskawatawa's magic more seriously.

Many did not scoff then when the Prophet placed a curse upon the American presidency. He went on to describe how Harrison, if he were to become the "Great Chief," would die in office. "And when he dies you will remember my brother Tecumseh's death," *The Haunting of the Presidents* quotes Tenskwatawa as saying. "And after him, every Great Chief chosen every twenty years thereafter will die. And when each one dies, let everyone remember the death of our people."

"Tippecanoe and Tyler Too!" was the campaign slogan that led William Henry Harrison to the White House in 1840. He departed his home in Cincinnati in late January of 1841 and was inaugurated March 4. Some say he caught his death of cold that day, but, whatever the case, four weeks later he became the first sitting U.S. president to die in office when he succumbed to pneumonia at the age of sixty-eight, a mere month after the inauguration. Tenskwatawa's prophecy was realized. William Henry

Harrison remains entombed in his presidential crypt on the banks of the Ohio River in North Bend, Ohio.

But, 166 years later, what of the Shawnee medicine man's "twenty-year curse"? History provides the startling answer:

- Abraham Lincoln—Elected in 1860, assassinated in 1865
- James Garfield—Elected in 1880, assassinated in 1881
- William McKinley—Elected in 1900, assassinated in 1901
- Warren G. Harding—Elected in 1920, died of illness less than three years into his first term in 1923
- Franklin Delano Roosevelt—Elected to a third term in 1940, died in office in 1945
- John F. Kennedy—Elected in 1960, assassinated in 1963
- Ronald Reagan—Elected in 1980, survived an assassination attempt in 1981

Although one might conclude this breaks the curse, there are those who surmise President Reagan's fatal Alzheimer's disease may have began during his final term as president. Martin and Birnes also suggest some parapsychologists believe the president may have survived John Hinckley, Jr.'s, assassination attempt because First Lady Nancy Reagan consulted astrological charts prior to the scheduling of all of the president's appointments. Mrs. Reagan has never publicly confirmed or denied this.

And what of President George W. Bush, elected in 2000? The answer might be found in a quote from Harvey Keitel, portraying Elvis in the 1999 film *Finding Graceland*: "One never knows what's fate or what's chance until the ride is over."

Cocktail Time for the General

I then began to ask them if they knew what he drank, what brand of whiskey he used, telling them most seriously that I wished they would find out. They conferred with each other and concluded they could not tell what brand he used. I urged them to ascertain and let me know, for if it made fighting generals like Grant I should like to get some of it for distribution.

—Abraham Lincoln to a delegation of congressmen urging him to fire Grant because he drank too much

Rumors of the great **Union General Ulysses S. Grant**'s fondness for brown whiskey on and off the battlefield are firmly implanted in historical lore. But did the man from the small town located where Big Indian Creek meets the Ohio River indeed battle the bottle?

Not long after newlyweds Jesse and Hannah Grant settled in the quiet little town of Point Pleasant, located on the north shore of the Ohio River in the southwest region of the Buckeye State in Clermont County, the couple's first son, Ulysses, was born on April 27, 1822. Jesse, the son of a ne'er-do-well alcoholic, had no tolerance for those not willing to stay sober and work hard. Dedicated to the ideals of earnest labor and proper education, when the time came, it seemed appropriate for Jesse Grant to procure an appointment for his eldest son to the United States Military Academy at West Point. Like many other cadets at the time, young Ulysses had his first exposure to alcohol here.

Early nineteenth-century Americans enjoyed their drink, consuming liquor because they believed it was nutritious,

General U.S. Grant

stimulated digestion, and relaxed the nerves. Potable spirits were also consumed to accompany food, which was often undercooked, greasy, salty, and sometimes rancid. When Grant graduated from West Point in 1843 and took his place as a second lieutenant in the small, professional army, drinking among the troops was widespread and generally accepted. The young officer took on the habit with his peers. He is known to have indulged frequently while serving in the Mexican War. By the time he returned from the war in 1848, he married and was assigned to an isolated garrison in New York Harbor, where he coped with boredom by hitting the bottle. By 1851, worried about his increasingly heavy drinking, Ulysses joined the Sons of Temperance and became an active participant in the temperance movement.

Transfers and different duties soon proved to be powerful motivators to lure Grant back to drinking. By 1853 the young officer found his assignment in Northern California so slow, tedious, and monotonous he found distraction by frequently drinking liquor with the boys at a local trading post. One night Grant apparently had one too many and appeared for duty under the influence. The post commander, Lt. Col. Robert Buchanan, strongly disapproved, instructing Grant to draft a letter of resignation to keep at hand. A short time later a similar instance of Grant's late-night hard drinking compelled Buchanan to give Grant the ultimatum of submitting the resignation or face a court-martial for being drunk on duty. Captain Grant chose the former.

Although drinking in the military was common and widely accepted in 1854, Grant was incautious about timing the instances where he indulged. On April 11 of that year, he tendered his resignation to the secretary of war. After fifteen years in the army, Grant returned to civilian life, where history shows he seemed to have little inclination or time to drink.

With the outbreak of the Civil War in 1861, Grant offered his services to the recently appointed commander of the Ohio Militia, Major General James B. McClellan. He received no response, so he made another offer to Brigadier General Nathaniel Lyon, who also did not respond. Evidently, Grant's reputation as a drunk preceded him.

Disappointed, Grant returned to his family tannery in Galena, Illinois, where he went about mustering volunteers into service. His efforts were noticed by an Illinois congressman who persuaded the state's governor to appoint the veteran West Point grad colonel of the 21st Illinois Infantry Regiment. The 21st had a reputation as a problem regiment, but Grant quickly whipped it into shape, a move that earned him a promotion to brigadier general by July 1861.

Jealousy ran deep among the ranks of command officers in the Union Army, and detractors fueled rumors of Grant's boozing that, according to them, had ended his previous military career. Although Grant did begin drinking again prior to the Battle of Shiloh in April 1862, there were no witnesses to validate he was drunk at the time. Despite the rumors, Grant forged on.

The most well-documented instances of the general's drinking habits came around May 1863 during the Union Army's siege of the Mississippi River port city of Vicksburg. The first happened on May 12, 1863, when a newspaper reporter, Sylvanus Cadwallader, attached himself to Grant's staff to follow the campaign. Cadwallader and Grant's chief of artillery, Colonel William Duff, were sitting inside Duff's tent when the general stepped in. Duff produced a cup and dipped it into a barrel he had stored in the tent. Grant emptied the contents and proceeded to guzzle down two refills. When Grant departed, Cadwallader learned the barrel contained whiskey.

Less than a month later, Cadwallader encountered General Grant aboard the steamboat *Diligence* on a cruise down the Yazoo River. "I was not long in perceiving that Grant had been drinking heavily," Cadwallader remembered, "and that he was still keeping it up. He made several trips to the bar room of the boat in a short time, and became stupid in speech and staggering in gait. This was the first time he had shown symptoms of intoxication in my presence, and I was greatly alarmed by his condition, which was fast becoming worse." According to Cadwallader, General Grant's drinking binge lasted two more days.

When Grant and several of his staff went to review the troops outside of New Orleans, shortly after the victory at Vicksburg, his horse stumbled and fell, and the general was injured. Rumors proliferated among the rank and file that the general was riding under the influence. Other examples, mere gossip or fact unknown, abound.

So, amidst the documented accounts, gossip and rumor that have found their way into history, was Ulysses S. Grant an alcoholic? Author James McPherson says, by today's standards, yes. But, in his book *Battle Cry of Freedom: The Civil War Era*, McPherson contends Grant's drinking habit may have actually *helped* in his famous military accomplishments:

> In the end ... his predisposition to alcoholism may have made him a better general. His struggle for self-discipline enabled him to understand and discipline others; the humiliation of pre-war failures gave him a quiet humility that was conspicuously absent from so many generals with a reputation to protect; because Grant had nowhere to go but up, he could act with more boldness and decision than commanders who dared not risk failure.

Abraham Lincoln's plan for distribution of cocktails to his military staff may have had more substance than mere presidential sarcasm.

The Fabulous Mayoral Massage

There once was a councilman named Springer
Who got a massage on his dinger.
He said, "Ah, what the heck?"

Then he wrote her a check ...
Now Springer's dinger's in the wringer.
—*Popular limerick around Cincinnati, circa 1974,
author unknown*

Gerald Norman "Jerry" Springer was born February
13, 1944, in London, England, to Margaret and Richard
Springer, Jewish refugees fleeing Nazi Germany. Upon gradu-
ating from law school in 1968, the young attorney became a
campaign aide to presidential hopeful Robert Kennedy. When
Kennedy was tragically felled by an assassin's bullet, Springer
found a home in Cincinnati, taking a position with the prominent law firm of Frost & Jacobs. Cincinnati also provided the
forum for Jerry's advancement in the world of politics.
Springer was known in the political world from his efforts
toward ratification of the Twenty-Sixth Amendment, the legis-
lation that granted eighteen-year-olds the right to vote. In
1970, Springer the newcomer surprised incumbent Republican
Congressman Donald Clancy, accumulating 45 percent of the
vote as a Democrat in a strongly Republican district.

In 1971, Springer was elected to his first term to Cincinnati
City Council. Then, in 1974, Springer abruptly ended his political career (he thought) when he became entangled in a prostitution scandal at a Northern Kentucky motel a couple miles
south of the Ohio River.

During a police raid of the "massage parlor," detectives
found a personal check, written and signed by Jerry Springer,
for "services rendered." The married young councilman
'fessed up publicly to his indiscretion and promptly resigned
from council. His honesty paid off apparently when he won a
council seat back by popular vote in 1975. He also served as
Cincinnati's mayor in 1977. Springer even used the sex scandal as part of his 1982 campaign to become the Democratic

Jerry Springer

candidate for Ohio governor. He used the incident to sell the idea he wasn't afraid to tell the truth, "even if it hurts." (The commercial was on YouTube in 2006.) Failing to win his party's nomination for governor, Jerry put his political career on hiatus. After stints as news anchor on Cincinnati's WLWT Channel 5 television station, Springer moved on to develop his "shock-TV program," *The Jerry Springer Show.*

Uncle Buz Feels His Oats

Buz Lukens was born in Harveysburg, Ohio, and attended school in Harveysburg and nearby Waynesville. He graduated from Ohio State University in 1954 before serving six and a half years in the United States Air Force, where he reached the rank of captain. His political career began in 1966 when he was elected to the United States House of Representatives, where he remained until 1970. He then left Washington to make a run for the Ohio governor's mansion. Losing the Republican primary election for governor, Lukens was elected to the Ohio State Senate where he stayed until he again won a national congressional seat in the 101st Congress.

As a U.S. congressman, Buz garnered unwanted national attention in 1989 when he was clandestinely filmed by an Ohio television station during a meeting at a Columbus-area McDonald's where he discussed, on camera, having sex with a Columbus-area teen with the sixteen-year-old's mother. Soon after footage of the meeting went public, Lukens was charged by a Franklin County grand jury with the misdemeanor of contributing to the delinquency of a minor for paying the youngster $40 and giving gifts in exchange for sexual favors. The grand jury ignored allegations that the affair began between Lukens and the girl when she was only thirteen.

On May 26, 1989, Buz was convicted by a jury in the Franklin County juvenile court. Though the state of Ohio's age of consent in such matters is sixteen, the congressman was convicted of a section that specifies, "No person shall ... aid, abet, induce, cause, encourage or contribute to a child or ward of the juvenile court into becoming an unruly or delinquent child." By his payment of $40 and gifts, the jury found Lukens abetting the child in the act of prostitution (paying another for sex acts).

The congressman appealed the conviction on the grounds the teenager was already delinquent by the time he had sex with her, which made her an unreliable witness. The *Columbus Dispatch* reported the appeals court's finding: "The appeals court discounted Thomas Tyack's (Lukens's attorney) contention that it was not possible to 'cause or contribute' to a child becoming unruly if the child was already unruly. Using an analogy, the court found that a person found guilty of polluting a river may not be the primary polluter but is still responsible for 'contributing' to the pollution."

Despite being rejected by the Republican Party, Lukens refused to resign his congressional office. In 1990 he lost the Republican primary in his congressional district to West Chester Republican John Boehner. But his problems weren't over. While Lukens was finishing his term on Capitol Hill, a Capitol Building elevator operator accused Buz of fondling her. The congressman finally resigned on October 24, 1990. He served nine days of a thirty-day jail sentence and was ordered to see a psychologist as well as submit to tests for sexually transmitted diseases.

A 1995 task force investigating a banking scandal in the House of Representatives also found cause to charge Buz Lukens with five counts of bribery and conspiracy for actions he took while representing Ohio in Congress. He was convicted of the charges in March 1996.

Beam Him Up, Scotty!

James Anthony Traficant, Jr., was born May 8, 1941, in Youngstown, Ohio. Educated with bachelor's and master's degrees from the University of Pittsburgh and another master's from Youngstown State University, he entered politics when he

Representative James Traficant

was elected sheriff of Mahoning County in 1981. While sheriff, Traficant received national media attention for refusing to execute foreclosure orders on several homes owned by locals who were unemployed due to the closure of steel mills in the area. The attention endeared him to the voting public, many of whom suffered because of the mill closings.

In 1983 Traficant was charged with racketeering under Ohio's Racketeer Influenced and Corrupt Organizations (RICO) laws for accepting bribes. He represented himself in the criminal trial and was acquitted, arguing that accepting the bribes was only his part of the ongoing corruption investigation. Actually using the publicity he garnered from the RICO trial, Traficant managed to get elected to the United States House of Representatives for Ohio's 17th District. He was reelected eight times.

James Traficant gained a reputation in Congress as being an eccentric, and he seemed to relish the image. His trademark closing when addressing the House was, "Beam me up ..." a reference to a *Star Trek* character who wanted to be "beamed" back to the spaceship from often unsavory locations.

In 2002, a federal indictment was brought against Traficant with charges of taking campaign funds for personal use. Insisting the charges were no more than a vendetta against him for acquittal in the 1983 trial, Jim again opted to represent himself. The national media paid special attention to the Traficant trial and frequently broadcast reports of the congressman's arguing with the judge and screaming at prosecutors and witnesses. On April 15, 2002, Jim Traficant was found guilty of ten felony counts, including bribery, racketeering, and tax evasion. Upon his conviction, the House Ethics Committee recommended expulsion from the House. On July 25, by a vote of 420 to 1, Congressman Traficant became the first member of the House in twenty-two years to be expelled.

Sentenced to eight years in the Federal Bureau of Prisons, Traficant wasn't ready to end his political career. While incarcerated, he ran as an independent candidate for another congressional term. His campaign was unsuccessful. Traficant remains in jail. His prison term ends in 2010.

For Official Government Use Only

When veteran Ohio **Senator Mike DeWine** fired a young woman from his office staff on May 21, 2004, for "unacceptable use of Senate computers," he was not trying to hide a scandal. He was not involved or even implicated in the "unacceptable use" and probably did not foresee the level of media attention the woman would ignite. But the attractive **Jessica Cutler**, whose age (twenty-four or twenty-six?) and credentials (Syracuse University grad or no?) are blurred, became the latest in a long line of young women drawn to Washington, D.C., where politically powerful men are drawn to them.

The debacle began when DeWine revealed one of his staff had used "resources and work time to post unsuitable and offensive material to an Internet Web log." Jessica's online "diary" was exceedingly graphic, implying that her sexual favors in return for money and gifts put her in a league with high-priced prostitutes. "Most of my living expenses are thankfully subsidized by a few generous older gentlemen," Cutler told the *Washington Post*. "I'm sure I am not the only one who makes money on the side this way. How can anybody live on $25K a year?"

After she was fired from her job, Cutler was candid with *Post* reporters. "If you don't like or care about your job," she told them, "what's the big deal? I am so over it. It's amazing to me that people have any interest in such a low-level sex scandal. If I were sleeping with a congressman, maybe, but I'm a nobody and the people writing about me are nobodies." She may have been "over it," but the press and several of her alleged lovers, who included high-ranking government officials, were not.

One senior DeWine staffer, Judiciary Committee counsel

Robert Steinbuch, objected to the online description by his "girlfriend" of their sexual escapades, which included notations that Steinbuch "liked spanking and disliked condoms," and "He likes talking dirty and stuff, and he told me he likes submissive women," Steinbuch took exception. He promptly sued Jessica for $20 million, claiming public humiliation. The case is currently pending.

Since Jessica was fired by Mike DeWine, she has moved to New York, where she wrote a novel, *The Washingtonienne*, based on the scandal. She also posed nude for *Playboy* magazine and started her own Web site where she solicits funds "for slutty clothes and drugs" (www.jessicacutleronline.com) As for the scandal itself, Cutler told the *Post* in 2004, "It's so clichéd. It's like, 'There's a slutty girl on the Hill?' There's millions of 'em. A lot of my friends are way worse than me."

As for Mike DeWine, he needed to look for a new job when Ohio voters elected Democrat Sherrod Brown to the U.S. Senate. Though his loss was due mostly to the Democratic wave of momentum resulting from the unpopular war in Iraq, it never helps a politician to be associated with a sex scandal, even when his association is limited to signing her paycheck.

Disorder in the Court!

Warren County **Judge Dallas Powers** received a dubious honor of sorts in 2005 when he became the first judge in Ohio to be charged with sex crimes in his own courtroom. CNN reported that the judge's defense attorney, John Smith, said Powers's troubles began in August of 2004 when a court employee walked into the judge's chambers to find Powers, then seventy-one, and a probation officer, Libbie Sexton, then thirty-four, in what appeared to be the beginning or end of a sex act. But, said Smith, the "open secret" affair between Powers and Sexton was not the cause of the investigation. "The complaints didn't come from the affair. It was because of the preferential treatment. The other employees didn't like that when there was overtime, Sexton got it or that she wore what she wanted at work."

Prosecutors saw the matter differently, and Judge Powers was originally charged with thirteen felony and three misdemeanor counts stemming from a variety of complaints about the judge's sexual antics at the courthouse, sexual harassment of female employees, intimidation, and favoritism. Eventually, prosecutors agreed to a plea bargain, and Powers pleaded guilty or no contest to two misdemeanors involving intimidation and preferential treatment of a public employee as well as three counts of public indecency. The judge was sentenced to three years probation and ineligibility to hold public office for seven years. "We're very pleased Dallas Powers will no longer be a judge in Ohio," Bob Beasley of the state attorney general's office told CNN, "and the employees are pleased he will not be able to set foot in the Warren County Courthouse again."

Not all of Powers's former employees were satisfied, however. Ten filed civil suits against Powers and the Warren County Board of Commissioners seeking damages for everything from sexual harassment (one plaintiff, Mary Velde, thirty-three, claimed in an affidavit Powers "placed his fingers in my vagina and his mouth on my breast") and verbal abuse to giving preferential treatment to Libbie Sexton.

Sexton, for her part, pleaded guilty to one count of attempted theft and no contest to two misdemeanors. "Essentially, she admitted doing homework for some college courses she was taking on a computer at work," Sexton's attorney, Chris Cornyn, told CNN. And her relationship with Dallas Powers? "She still considers him a friend today." Good friends?

Guilty on "Fore" Counts

Ohio politics have almost always involved the Taft name. Such was the case in August 2005 when **Governor Bob Taft** drew the attention of the national media. But this time it wasn't the usual news that Bob's father and grandfather, both U.S. senators, or his great-grandfather, William Howard Taft, who served as both president and chief justice of the Supreme Court, experienced. No, this time the Republican was being noticed for becoming the first Ohio governor in the state's history to be convicted of a crime by admitting to four misdemeanor counts of ethics violations for failing to report fifty-two golf outings, dinners, and other entertainment gifts.

"No one is above the law in the state of Ohio," Franklin County Municipal Court Judge Mark Froelich told the governor after the guilty plea, adding that as governor, Taft had a duty to "set an example for all citizens." "I'm very disappointed in myself," Taft told the judge before he was fined $4,000. Perhaps most disturbing about the charges against Governor Taft was the fact they were linked to a larger investigation, that of Tom Noe, a Republican fund-raiser who managed a $50 million rare coin investment for the Ohio Bureau of Worker's Compensation. Approximately $13 million of the investment was missing. Noe took control of $25 million in 1998 and another $25 million was entrusted to him on July 26, 2002, five days after Noe played golf with Governor Taft.

Noe was eventually found guilty of stealing $2 million for his personal use and of money laundering, forgery, and corrupt activity involving the rare coin fund scandal. In November of 2006 he was sentenced to eighteen years in the state prison and

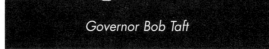

Governor Bob Taft

ordered to pay fines and restitution.

Bob Taft refused to resign from the governor's office after his conviction. Because of term limitations, he was ineligible to run again in 2006. Democrat Ted Strickland soundly defeated the Republican candidate. Perhaps Governor Bob Taft's most enduring legacy as Ohio's chief executive can be found in his post-sentencing court statement: "There are no words to express the deep remorse that I feel over the embarrassment that I have caused for my administration and for the people of the state of Ohio. I offer my sincere and heartfelt apology, and I hope the people will understand that these mistakes, though major and important mistakes, were done unintentionally, and I hope and pray they will accept my apology."

THE BUCKEYE STATE

PSYCHO
KILLER

HALL OF FAME

15

QUIET, RURAL AND SERENE? CONSERVATIVE
Midwest? Hardly. Ohio has seen more than its
share of vicious wackos who seem to prey upon
the innocent. The following are the worst Ohio
has to offer. The worst and then some. Consider
if you will, in no particular order …

Can I Get You a Beer?
Just Say "No" to Arsenic Anna

Anna Hahn immigrated to Cincinnati from her native Germany in 1929. The former Munich schoolteacher arrived in America with her son and husband, a Vienna doctor. The doctor died soon after their arrival. Anna decided to stay in the States and settled in the mostly German immigrant Over-the-Rhine section of Cincinnati where she had relatives. In her early thirties, the plump, yet attractive, blond met telegraph operator Philip Hahn, and the two married. Shortly thereafter, Philip quit his telegraph job, and the Hahns opened two delicatessens to earn their way.

When Anna first came to Cincinnati, she had moved in with her aunt and uncle who owned a house on Cincinnati's Colerain Avenue. When the elderly relatives died, shortly after Anna's arrival, the niece and her new family moved into the residence. By all outward appearances, Anna Hahn became a typical Midwest housewife. It wasn't until she decided to travel to Colorado on a train that her true dark nature began to expose itself.

Hahn and her son Oskar had checked into a Colorado Springs hotel with an elderly man named George Obendorfer on July 30, 1937. By August 1, Obendorfer was dead, having been rushed to a hospital after contracting a sudden illness. Anna and Oskar had split town by the time local police traced the dead man back to his hotel. They did notice George's companions' names on the register, though. They also discovered the hotel proprietor was investigating the apparent theft of $300 in jewelry. It didn't take long before the authorities alerted Cincinnati police, Anna Hahn was wanted in Colorado. Cincinnati detectives obligingly picked Mrs. Hahn up, and pieces of an ugly puzzle fell together.

Anna began various tales of her trip to the Rockies with George Obendorfer, and her inconsistencies caused the already suspicious police to dig deeper. Soon a series of untimely deaths of older "friends" of Anna Hahn emerged. Jacob Wagner, Olive Koehler and her sister Mary Arnold, George Gsellman, George Heis—all seemed to be in perfectly good health until they accepted gifts of ice cream or refreshing beer from Anna Hahn and mysteriously became sick and died. Coincidence and circumstance became less and less likely.

An unlikely witness came forth in person as Philip Hahn produced a bottle of the poisonous liquid croton oil, which he said he confiscated from his wife after recognizing symptoms of poisoning in his own body. Croton oil was a drug available at most pharmacies at the time. A large amount used in a short time usually proved fatal, especially to the elderly or infirm. The human body breaks down croton oil swiftly, which would make its detection difficult during a perfunctory autopsy. Philip seized the bottle marked "Croton Oil Poison X" from Anna upon discovering it in her possessions after a spell where he felt uncharacteristically sick. He kept it in his locker at work, intending to turn it over to police in the event "anything happened."

The more police looked, the more "suspicious" deaths they associated with Anna Marie Hahn. There was Albert Palmer, a seventy-two-year-old with a fondness for horse racing. Palmer died of a mysterious heart attack in 1936 after visiting, as he often did, a "betting establishment" with Anna in the Cincinnati suburb of Elmwood Place. Palmer's relatives reported Albert as often looking "doped" after attending sessions with Mrs. Hahn. The untimely deaths of Anna's aunt and uncle, Mr. and Mrs. Johannes Oswald, shortly after Anna's arrival in Cincinnati also raised a red flag.

By August 10, 1937, Hamilton County prosecutors felt

HEARTLESS!
"Arsenic Anna" Hahn

they had enough. Anna Marie Hahn was indicted for the poisoning murder of Jacob Wagner. The state put on a strong case, offering money as the prime motive for the murder. Anna's defense strategy seemed lame as denial was all the defense offered, declaring the prosecutor's case was "lies, all lies."

Prosecutors portrayed Mrs. Hahn as a heartless murderer:

> She is sly because she developed her relationships with old men who had no relatives and lived alone. She is avaricious, because no act was so low that she wasn't ready to commit it for slight gain. She is cold-blooded, like no other woman in the world, because no one could sit here for four weeks and hear this parade of evidence and display no emotion. She is heartless, because nobody with a heart could deal out a death she dealt to those old men. We've seen here the coldest, most heartless cruel person that ever has come within the scope of our lives.

The prosecutor called on the dead to conclude his closing argument:

> In the four corners of this courtroom stand four dead men. Gsellman, Palmer, Wagner, Obendorfer! From the four corners bony fingers point at her and they say, "That woman poisoned me! That woman made my last moments an agony! That woman tortured me with the tortures of the damned!" And then, turning to you they say, "Let my death be not entirely in vain. My life cannot be brought back, but through my death and the punishment to be inflicted upon her, you can prevent such a death from coming to another old man." From the four corners of this courtroom, those old men say to you "Do your duty!" I ask of you, for the state of Ohio, that you withhold any recommendation of mercy.

Indeed, the jury withheld "mercy." On December 7, 1938, after a series of appeals, Anna Hahn became the first woman in Ohio history to go to the electric chair. She didn't go quietly. Begging for mercy, she was strapped into "Ol' Sparky" and electrocuted. She was officially pronounced dead at 8:13 p.m. The next day she was buried in unconsecrated ground at the Holy Cross Catholic Cemetery in Columbus. A few days later her portrait was added to those of the other 213 previously electrocuted by the state.

Anna managed to speak from the grave in a series of letters she arranged to sell to the *Cincinnati Enquirer* prior to her execution. Proceeds from the letters were to go to an education fund for her son, Oskar. Hahn confessed and offered remedial explanations for the murders in her writing.

"I don't know how I could have done the things I did in my life," Anna wrote. "Only God knows what came over me when I gave Albert Palmer that first one, the poison that caused his death. ... When I stood by Mr. Wagner as he was laid out at the funeral home don't know how it was that I didn't scream out at the top of my voice. I couldn't believe that it was me. ... I can't believe it even today."

Anna went on to portray disbelief and remorse for her actions. Genuine or not, only she knows. What is not in dispute is Anna Marie Hahn has the distinction of being a serial killer fifty years before the term was ever coined. She also goes into Ohio history as the first of only three women to be executed in the state's electric chair.

Malpractice and Murder Medical Specialist

Mike Swango seemed a promising medical student in 1983 when, freshly graduated from Southern Illinois University, he began a medical residency at the distinguished Ohio State University Medical Center in Columbus. But if the Swango saga is true, Dr. Swango could be the most proficient serial killer of all time, leaving an intercontinental headcount in his wake that lasted from his days at OSU in 1983 to a stunning conclusion in 1997. The numbers vary on a suspected death total, but estimates range from thirty-five to sixty. James B. Stewart, author of *Blind Eye: The Terrifying Story of a Doctor Who Got Away with Murder*, blames the American hospital administration system for failure to detect and put an end to Swango's reign of mass-murder-medicine despite red flags thrown by nurses and patients alike at most of the institutions where Swango practiced.

Despite some questionable events in Mike Swango's behavior at SIU, which included delayed graduation, he accepted an offer to participate in a neurosurgery residency at prestigious Ohio State in July of 1983. The only person selected out of sixty applicants, Swango found himself as one of 4,278 employees at the 1,123 bed hospital, which reigned supreme nationally and statewide with other teaching hospital giants like the Cleveland Clinic, Case Western Reserve, and the University of Cincinnati.

By January of 1984, young Dr. Swango was having problems with his general residency at Ohio State, including a complaint from a supervising physician about Swango's remarks suggesting a fascination with Nazis and the Holocaust. It wasn't until then, says author James B. Stewart, that the director of Ohio State's neurosurgery department, Dr. William Hunt, contacted SIU's associate dean for medical education, Howard Barrows, and inquired, "What kind of guy did you send us?" Barrows confirmed problems with Swango that had been mentioned in the SIU dean's letter sent to OSU, to which Hunt replied, "I don't read dean's letters." To Dr. Hunt's dismay, he learned of the comments in the dean's letter after locating a copy, a little over six months after hiring Swango.

Still, Michael Swango maintained his position in Columbus, being assigned to the ninth floor of a wing of the hospital known as Rhodes Hall. The death rate on Swango's floor increased startlingly. Other doctors, nurses, even patients noticed unusual and disturbing things occurring when Dr. Swango showed up, usually alone and often for no logical reason. News of mysterious deaths, all of which took place in the presence of Dr. Swango, soon reached Ohio State University's top administrators.

Fearing a scandal that would trump an important fund-raising campaign, officials of the medical school elected to assign Dr. Joseph Goodman, a professor of neurosurgery who had performed the surgery on one of Swango's alleged victims, to investigate internally. Goodman's investigation was three-fold. First he interviewed Rena Cooper, a sixty-nine-year-old woman who had undergone a lower back operation the morning before she fell into suspicious cardiac arrest. She was eventually resuscitated to the point where she identified Swango as the man who injected something into her IV before she became paralyzed. Swango denied having any contact with Cooper.

The rest of Goodman's investigation consisted of a review of files on several deceased patients and examining the results of a blood test conducted on Rena Cooper. He did not interview any of the medical personnel on the scene of the deaths. Nor did he order autopsy or toxicology reports on the bodies of purported victims. Goodman's report to the committee suggested there was no reason to further investigate Michael Swango or dismiss him from Ohio State. When concerned personnel insisted on pursuing the charges, an even more cursory "quiet inquiry" into the matter took place. Swango was reinstated without further investigation.

The day after Swango was assigned to Doane Hall after a routine rotation, the unusual deaths started happening again. Mystified physicians could not explain fatal blood clots, excessive bleeding resembling a fatal snakebite like that of a poisonous cobra, or the death of a twenty-two-year-old who was apparently recovering satisfactorily from surgery. When Swango bought three co-workers and himself fast food chicken dinners one day, everyone but him became violently ill for a week. Still, Dr. Swango completed his general surgery rotation and was transferred to Columbus Children's Hospital.

Summer arrived and Mike Swango returned to Illinois, where he took a paramedic job at a local hospital. A pattern soon developed wherein his co-workers compared bizarre stories of Swango boasting about his enjoyment of violent death and victim's last moments in this world. The co-workers noted an eerie undertone to a lot of Swango's stories up to and including his description of "coming out of the operating room with a hard-on to tell parents their child had died." When a group of paramedics took turns on different occasions accepting food and drink from Mike Swango, they set up a test that confirmed arsenic poisoning had caused the illness. Swango was arrested and charged with battery.

A search of Swango's apartment revealed, according to an Adams County Sheriff's Office report, an "entire mini-lab set up. ... Detectives found numerous chemicals, suspected poisons and poisonous compounds. Underground type magazines were observed that gave technical information on exotic poisons. ... Handwritten recipes for poisons and poisonous compounds were observed." There was an assortment of guns and knives and, perhaps most disturbing, books on the occult like *The Book of Ceremonial Magic, The Necronomicon,* and *The Modern Witch's Spell Book,* along with handwritten spells, incantations, and items with peculiar markings.

Meanwhile, Ohio State University was awaiting Swango's return when they received news of his arrest in the form of an inquiry on the young resident's background. The request came from Illinois authorities as part of their investigation of the Quincy paramedics' poisoning. Ohio State authorities tried to avoid the issue again, but the media forced an investigation causing Ohio State to admit it had harbored a fiend. With a new investigation of Swango's activity ignited, Ohio State severed ties with the graduated intern. Or did it?

Despite the growing investigation and the charges in Quincy, Swango applied for a job as an ER physician in northern Ohio with National Emergency Service in Toledo. Still licensed in Ohio, Swango had made no mention of his arrest or pending trial. Although Ohio State was now investigating Swango and knew about the Illinois charges, it still provided National Emergency Service with a certificate showing Swango had completed his internship at Ohio State. In short order, Dr. Swango was back in business at Fisher-Titus Memorial Hospital in Huron County.

On April 20, 1985, Mike Swango finally went on trial for the poisoning of co-workers in Quincy, Illinois. He was found guilty of six of seven counts of aggravated battery. A pre-sentence investigation noted how difficult it was to get information from Ohio State. Even after the convictions, all Ohio State would say was, "An incident occurred whereby a patient on a floor he was working on had a 'respiratory arrest.' The patient was placed in intensive care for one day. His supervisor told him to take two days off, away from the floor."

Sentencing day came, bringing a collection of witnesses speaking for and against Swango. For his part, Swango asserted his innocence before pleading for mercy. Judge Dennis Cashman was unimpressed; he gave Swango the maximum sentence, five years, saying, "You deserve the maximum under the law because there is no excuse for what you have done."

Feeling the convictions solidified evidence against Swango at Ohio State, the Franklin County prosecutor's office pursued an investigation in Columbus. The prosecutor hired veteran homicide investigator Patrick McSweeney to work the Swango case. But McSweeney found OSU a difficult place to work. As the detective later told author James B. Stewart:

> Everyone on the OSU staff was hesitant. Appointments were broken. We made it as convenient as possible. We'd go in at 2:00 a.m. if that's what they wanted. Not one of them showed up on time. Once we waited three hours for a doctor to show up. They sent some doctors away [out of town] when we wanted them. I got the impression that they thought we were just dumb cops and they were the saviors of mankind. I've dealt with hospitals for years on homicides, and I've never seen anything compared to the treatment we got at OSU.

Despite the difficulty, investigators eventually managed to study the records of every death occurring at the hospital during Dr. Swango's rotations. They isolated five suspicious deaths plus strange illnesses of doctors who ate lunch with Swango during his stint at Children's Hospital. Officials at Ohio State continued to thwart the investigation. With only circumstantial evidence, albeit strong circumstantial evidence, against Swango, the Ohio State cases stalled.

On August 21, 1987, Mike Swango was released by the

Illinois Department of Corrections after serving only two years of his five-year sentence. He relocated to Newport News, Virginia, this time and even applied for a Virginia medical license. Fortunately he was rejected. Other jobs came and went and, true to form, fellow employees at one of his jobs fell sick, indeed almost died, from food poisoning.

But Mike Swango still wanted to be Dr. Swango, so he continued applying at medical centers across the country. Amazingly, Swango managed to lie his way into a position at the University of South Dakota in Sioux Falls. But his luck ran out when he applied for membership in the American Medical Association even though he was an unlicensed doctor who had obtained an internship through deceit. The AMA conducted a thorough background check while, coincidentally, ABC re-aired a 1986 segment of *20/20* in which reporter John Stossel interviewed Swango at Illinois's Centralia Correctional. In the interview Swango impied that he purposely injected doughnuts with ant poison. Another gig up, this time at USD.

It seems incredible, but the exposure in South Dakota may have been a mere annoyance for Swango. He managed to get another residency, this time in psychiatry at the State University of New York at Stony Brook. At the new resident's first assignment at a VA hospital on Long Island, Swango's first patient died mysteriously only hours after Swango's arrival. It didn't take long until authorities began to piece together the puzzle that was their misplaced trust, combined with a degree of negligence, to take a closer look at Michael Swango. He, as always it seemed, once again disappeared.

After showing up in Georgia and Florida, Swango felt some heat. As usual he fled, this time to Africa, where his murderous rampage continued. By the time African authorities caught up, Swango had been involved in more "suspicious deaths." He traveled back to the States, where he was apprehended by INS

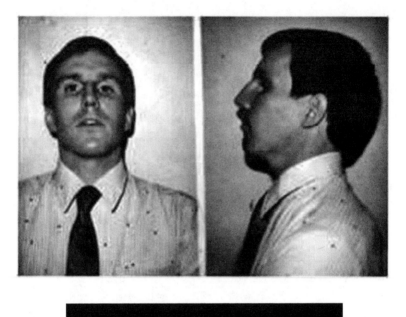

Michael Swango

agents at Chicago's O'Hare airport and charged federally with fraud and practicing medicine without a license. This allowed the FBI to build cases in the suspicious deaths.

In 1998 Michael Swango, in an effort to prevent extradition to Africa, pleaded guilty to three counts of homicide occurring while he was at the VA in New York. He also pleaded guilty to the poisoning by potassium of the young gymnast Cynthia McGee in 1983. McGee's death was never satisfactorily explained to some at the time. The cursory and inept investigation conducted by the Ohio State medical administrators and staff, in retrospect, perhaps, could've been the precursor to a murder spree that killed dozens.

.22 Terror Times in Columbus

In the early-morning hours of December 10, 1977, the bullet-riddled bodies of thirty-seven-year-old Joyce Vermillion and thirty-three-year-old Karen Dodrill were found frozen in a snow bank outside Forker's Café, a local bar in Newark, forty miles east of Columbus in Ohio's Licking County. A pile of .22 caliber shell casings littered the scene. As the media would later dub the affair, the ".22 Caliber Killings" had begun.

The Newark killings seemed to be solved early when a twenty-six-year-old go-go dancer confessed to local police she had witnessed the shootings, which were perpetrated by her boyfriend and an accomplice shortly after the bar closed at 2:30 a.m. on the frigid December night. Unfortunately, her confession turned out to be a hoax.

A little over two months later, on February 12, 1978, fifty-two-year-old Mickey McCann; his mother, seventy-seven-year-old Dorothy McCann; and Mickey's girlfriend, twenty-six-year-old Christine Herdman, were found dead in the McCann home in their semirural home in Franklin County just outside the Columbus city limits. Telephone lines to the house were cut and among the carnage in the house investigators found a scatter of .22 shell casings around the bodies. Herdmann had suffered multiple gunshots in her right cheek, right shoulder, and forehead, Dorothy McCann had wounds to her mouth, head, and right leg, and Mickey had at least five shots to the head.

A sixth murder attributed to a .22 occurred on April 8, 1978, when seventy-seven-year-old Jenkin Jones was found shot six times in his rural Granville, Ohio, home. Once again, multiple .22 cartridge shell casings were found at the crime scene near Denison University just outside of Newark. Just weeks after, on April 30, a security guard, Gerald Fields, was found murdered at a private club southeast of Columbus in Fairfield County. Fields, too, lay among spent .22 caliber shell casings.

Detectives submitted the casings and bullets recovered from all of the murder scenes to the crime lab for comparison. The evidence proved a grim reality when casings from each scene matched; a serial killer was at work in central Ohio. Still, there was no clear indication of motive, much less a viable suspect to pursue. Law enforcement was stymied.

Three weeks later, on May 21, forty-seven-year-old Jerry Martin and his fifty-year-old wife, Martha, were found by a relative in their Franklin County home, both suffering multiple gunshot wounds. Once again the telltale casings were left behind. They matched casings found at the other crimes. Upon inspection, the casings from Forker's Café matched also. The go-go dancer and company were jailed during the later crimes, proving a false confession. Police were back to square one on all of the .22 caliber killings.

By November 1978 the killings stopped. Authorities speculated one of three possibilities existed:

The killer(s) were convicted of some other crime and had been incarcerated.

The killer(s) were scared off by investigators getting "too close."

There was a connection among all of the victims that had been negated by the final murders.

When no apparent link could be found, investigators turned to the offer of a $16,000 reward for information on the murderers. The cash brought dozens of calls to the Columbus police. But, after more than 250 tips and weeks of investigation, authorities were no closer to the killers.

The quiet ended abruptly on December 4, 1978, when Columbus resident Joseph Annick, age fifty-six, was shot five times in his chest and stomach while working in his garage. Although .22 casings were found at the scene, tests proved they were from a different weapon than was used in the previous crimes. But the modus operandi was crystal clear—the .22 killer had struck again.

A huge break came five days after Annick's murder when a man was picked up at a Columbus department store trying to use Annick's credit card. Thirty-eight-year-old **Gary Lewingdon** was promptly arrested and questioned by detectives.

Lewingdon, a Vietnam veteran with a history of petty crimes including theft, indecent exposure, possession of criminal tools, and concealed weapons charges, had lived with his mother until marrying and moving with his wife in 1977 to Kirkersville, Ohio, where he started a job with Rockwell International as a repairman. Kirkersville is the midpoint between Columbus and Newark and Granville, Ohio.

Detectives were mildly surprised when, upon questioning, Lewingdon freely admitted murdering Joe Annick. He also willingly implicated himself in the nine other slayings. Not only that, he identified his partner in the crimes as his brother, forty-two-year-old **Thaddeus Lewingdon**. Thaddeus was promptly picked up.

Like Gary, Thaddeus was happy to recount the murders in graphic detail. According to the elder Lewingdon, Gary would select the victims, and the two would don ski masks and gloves, fit their .22 caliber pistol with a homemade silencer, then go about the crime. Thaddeus said it was easy until the Martin murders began to weigh on his mind. The two had a falling out prior to the Annick murder, which Thaddeus blamed solely on Gary. On December 14 both brothers were indicted by a Franklin County grand jury. Gary faced twenty felony counts, ten for murder, while Thaddeus drew seventeen counts, nine for murder.

Both brothers were convicted and received multiple life terms in Ohio penitentiaries. Gary lost his mind after his trial, was declared psychotic, and was transferred to the state hospital for the criminally insane. After their initial interrogations, the Lewingdon brothers never spoke in graphic terms of their murder spree again. A certain motive was never determined.

Despite an escape attempt in 1982, Gary Lewingdon remains in state custody. In 1983 Gary petitioned a Hamilton County court for permission to commit suicide—his request was denied. Gary currently resides at the Southern Ohio Correctional Facility in Lucasville. At age fifty-two, Thaddeus Lewingdon died in prison of lung cancer.

A Grim Hunting Season

The gently rolling hills and wide-open spaces of southeastern Ohio's mostly rural counties are a sportsman's paradise. During hunting and fishing season the ample streams and forests provide a peaceful atmosphere for those wanting to escape the congested rat race of big-city life. Locals enjoy the quiet life in small communities and family farms. Such was the case for young Jamie Paxton, a twenty-one-year-old who lived with his parents in the sleepy town of Bannock, Ohio. November 10, 1990, was a crisp, cool Saturday in Bannock and Jamie's day off from his weekday job as a steelworker. Deer season for crossbow hunters had arrived in Ohio, so Jamie rose early, breakfasted with his mother, and headed to the now gold/red late-autumn woods and pastures in the hope of bagging some venison.

Around 3:00 p.m., Jamie's mother, forty-nine-year-old Jean Paxton, expected her son's car to pull into the driveway any minute. With luck, in the trunk there would be the day's prize of a buck deer. It seemed eerily odd to Mrs. Paxton then when a sheriff's patrol car stopped in front of their house instead. Every parent's worst nightmare struck the Paxtons as the deputy described how Jamie had been found by friends along Ohio Route 9, shot in the chest, right knee, and buttocks. His death couldn't have been a hunting accident—not with multiple gunshot wounds, especially during bow season.

Police investigators studied every angle. They interviewed, even polygraphed, Jamie's friends, family members, and acquaintances. When they reached a dead end in the investigation, they were baffled. "Everyone in the area knew Jamie Paxton," said Sheriff Tom McCort. "No one that we knew of had ever disliked the young man." The seemingly senseless murder sent shockwaves of fear through the region.

By October of 1991 the murder of Jamie Paxton was quickly reaching cold-case status. Jean Paxton, more than anything else, wanted answers. In an effort to reach the killer, she began a letter-writing campaign and had her messages published in the *Martin's Ferry Times Leader* newspaper:

To the murderer(s) of my son, Jamie, would it be easier for you if I wrote words of hate? I can't because I don't feel hate. I feel deep sorrow at losing my son. You took a light from my life November 10 and left me with many days of darkness. Have you thought of your own death? Unless you confess your sin and ask for God's forgiveness, you will face the fire and fury of hell. When you are caught, I will be sorry for your family. They will have to carry the burden of your guilt all their lives.

Most felt the murderer was a callous, ruthless monster who would be unmoved by Jean's pleas. Some felt the killer may even be amused. But Jean persisted:

It's been nearly a year since you killed my son. Has your life changed in the last 11 months? Our family hasn't lived since last November 10. We are surviving one day at a time. There is one question on our minds all day long and every time we wake up at night: we want to know why Jamie was killed?

Mrs. Paxton's efforts were not in vain. The killer replied in an anonymous typewritten letter addressed to the *Times Leader*, the Paxtons, and Sheriff McCort. He qualified himself by delivering details of the murder that were not made public. His chilling confession read:

> I am the murderer of Jamie Paxton. Jamie Paxton was a complete stranger to me. I never saw him before in my life, and he never said a word to me that Saturday. Paxton was killed because of an irresistible compulsion that has taken over my life. I knew when I left my house that day that someone would die by my hand. I just didn't know who or where. Technically, I meet the definition of a serial killer, but I'm an average looking person with a family, job and home just like yourself.
>
> Something in my head causes me to turn into a merciless killer with no conscience. To the Paxtons, you deserve to know the details.
>
> I was very drunk and a voice inside my head said, "do it." I stopped my car behind Jamie's and got out. Jamie started walking very slowly down the hill toward the road. He appeared to be looking at something past me in the distance.
>
> I raised my rifle to my shoulder and lined him up in the sights. It took at least five seconds to take careful aim. My first shot was off a little bit and hit him in

the right chest. He groaned and went down. I wanted to make sure he was finished so I fired a second shot aimed half-way between his hip and shoulder. He was crawling around on the ground. I jerked the shot and hit him in the knee. He raised his head and groaned again. My third shot also missed and hit him in the butt. He never moved again.

Five minutes after I shot Paxton, I was drinking a beer and had blocked out all of my thoughts of what I had just done out of my mind. I thought no more of shooting Paxton than shooting a bottle at the dump.

I know you hate my guts, and rightfully so. I think about Jamie every hour of the day, as I am sure you do. Don't feel bad about not solving the case. You could interview until doomsday everyone that Jamie Paxton ever met in his life and you wouldn't have a clue to my identity. With no motive, no weapon, and no witnesses you could not possibly solve this crime.

The letter was signed "The Murderer of Jamie Paxton."

A mother's love and her antipathy for his murderer exposed a serial killer nobody knew was walking among us. The Belmont County sheriff's office now had its first lead. But the killer's message bore another grim reality: he would have to strike again before the scent could be detected on his trail.

Peace returned to the Ohio hills until another Saturday in March 1992. Claude Hawkins, a forty-nine-year-old married father of four who worked the night shift at a local factory, decided to spend the beginning of his morning off trying his luck fishing at his favorite spot below Will's Creek Dam just northwest of Belmont, Ohio, in Coshocton County. The quiet cove became a murder scene when other fishermen discovered Claude's body, shot in the back at close range, lying on the Will's Creek bank.

Will's Creek Dam is located on property owned by the federal government, making the Hawkins murder a federal matter. FBI Special Agent Harry Trumbitis, of the Columbus office, was assigned to the case. Trumbitis knew they were dealing with a peculiar brand of criminal when searches for a shell casing or other evidence proved fruitless. He was also convinced Claude Hawkins's death was not an isolated event.

Two weeks later, on March 26, 1992, officers from four Ohio counties, the Ohio Division of Wildlife, and the Federal Bureau of Investigation met in New Philadelphia, Ohio, just south of Canton, to compare notes.

Gruesome similarities pointed to an April 1, 1989, early-morning murder of a jogger on the back roads of Tuscarawas County as possibly the first in an emerging pattern of senseless killings. The jogger, Donald Welling, a thirty-five-year-old truck driver, had been jogging along a rural highway when he was shot through the heart by a .30 caliber bullet fired from about ten feet away. At the time, Tuscarawas County (approximately one hundred miles north of Belmont County) could not find any motive or evidence in the matter.

The connection to Jamie Paxton's death seemed apparent. Investigators surmised Welling's killer was inactive for the nineteen months before he struck Jamie Paxton. They also concluded that the "hunting accident" death of thirty-year-old Kevin Loring while deer hunting in a strip mine area of Muskingum County (west of Belmont and south of Coshocton counties), eighteen days after Jamie's shooting, on November 28, 1990, was very likely related. Loring, married and the father of three, had been found with a single gunshot wound to the face. Pieces of the twisted serial killer's puzzle were falling into place. Then, just ten days after the New Philadelphia conference, the serial killer struck another outdoorsman. Gary Bradley, a forty-four-year-old West Virginia steelworker, was found shot in the back while fishing in Noble County, adjacent to Belmont County. An emergency task force of law enforcement officials from five Ohio counties and the FBI was established. Not wanting to alert the murderer, the task force remained secret.

The task force met in early May 1992 at the FBI field office in Columbus. Officers of the five counties presented details of their individual investigations. Also on hand were representatives of the FBI's Behavioral Sciences Unit. Also known as the "Hannibal Lecter Squad," the unit specializes in developing "personality profiles" of serial killers. In this case, the profilers surmised:

> The suspect is a white male over thirty, a gun enthusiast, avid hunter and owns at least several weapons. The killer has above-average intelligence but is introverted and without many friends, and will resolve personal problems in a cowardly fashion. He might have a drinking problem and engage in obscene telephone calls, arson fire and vandalism by shooting out windows or tires of vehicles. He likely takes sadistic delight in mutilating and killing animals of all sorts. Stressful events would trigger his criminal episodes, which usually are committed while he is drunk.

The profile concluded the killer "lives within easy driving distance of the slayings."

By mid-summer the task force had ruled out at least a hundred potential suspects. The trail cooled once again, and once again, Jean Paxton took to the newspaper in hopes of contacting the killer. July 30, 1992, on what would have been Jamie Paxton's twenty-third birthday, the *Times Leader* ran Mrs. Paxton's letter describing how she had baked her son a cake. "But Jamie wasn't there to enjoy it," she wrote. "There's a small child in our family whose biggest worry was 'who's going to blow out the candles on Jamie's cake?' ... The next time there's a birthday party in your family I hope you think of the cake on our table and know you are the reason Jamie wasn't there to blow out the candles."

The letter went unanswered. Authorities figured the murderer feared sending another response. By August, the task force went public with a press release. The *Cleveland Plain Dealer* ran a headline: "Slayings Linked in Rural Ohio." The ensuing article reported the deaths of five sportsmen in a loose cluster of eastern Ohio counties. It went on to say the murders were suspected to be the work of a lone serial sniper. The *Plain Dealer* also published a copy of the FBI's suspect profile.

The media attention provided a break. On August 11, 1992, forty-three-year-old Richard Fry called the Tuscarawas County sheriff's office after reading about the murders in the *Plain Dealer*. "I saw reports about the task force that had been formed to solve the killings," Fry told Detective Walter Wilson. "I just think I got a guy who should be investigated as a possible suspect." Wilson met with Fry the same day.

At the meeting Fry explained to the detective that the profile fit an old high school buddy of his, **Tom Dillon**. Fry recalled how he and Dillon would cruise around rural Ohio in the 1970s drinking beer, shooting at road signs, and sometimes lighting small fires. Fry later recounted to reporters from the *Akron Beacon Journal* tales of driving the Ohio countryside when Dillon produced a gun to shoot at dogs he noticed along the roadway. "Those are somebody's pets," Fry says he told

Dillon. "Somebody loves them. It's just not right to do that."

"Once, while driving back from Atwood Lake in Carroll County," Fry told the *Beacon Journal*, "Tom pulled off the side of the road and pulled out this gun and started shooting at this farmer. Apparently, the farmer was a good ways off—two, three hundred yards. One of the others in the car protested, 'What the hell are you doing?' Dillon explained that he couldn't hit a target at that distance with a pistol, so I'm just 'plinking at him.'" Fry claims he broke off their association.

Years later, in 1986, Fry says he ran into Dillon again in Newcomerstown in southern Tuscarawas County. Dillon explained his presence by saying he was "... just driving around, this and that." Fry was suspicious, believing Dillon was traveling further south because he was still up to his old ways. Despite his reservations, Fry agreed to ride with Dillon to a Cleveland area gun collector's show. During the drive, Fry said in news accounts, Dillon made numerous disturbing comments during conversation.

"I remember one time," Fry says about Dillon, "he and I were driving and he said, 'Do you realize you can go out into the country and find somebody and there are no witnesses? You can shoot them. There is no motive. Do you realize how easy murder would be to get away with?'"

On another occasion Fry says Dillon talked about a fascination with serial killer Ted Bundy and how he succeeded in murder without getting caught. "Do you think I've ever killed anybody?" Fry says Dillon asked him. When Fry responded "no," he says Dillon told him, "That just proves you don't know me very well." Tom Dillon's address was in Magnolia, Ohio, about seventy-five miles from the site where Jamie Paxton was murdered.

Detectives began to delve into Thomas Dillon's past. A check on Dillon's firearms purchases revealed he owned numerous rifles and handguns he had purchased from a licensed dealer. The dealer's records showed Dillon had bought eighteen weapons in the past couple years, including two rifles of the type used on four of the five sportsmen.

A close look at Dillon indicated a stellar work record of twenty-two years. His criminal contacts proved more interesting. In 1969, while a student at Ohio State University, Dillon was found to be in possession of a Russian mortar grenade launcher. Authorities considered the weapon more of a collector's item than anything and no charges were pursued. A more recent 1991 incident attracted the detective's attention. In August of that year, Dillon was cited by a state game warden for illegal target practice near an Ohio hunting reserve in southern Stark County. During a search of his truck, the warden seized a .22 caliber pistol equipped with an illegal silencer. Dillon had pleaded guilty to the silencer charge and was awaiting final sentencing at the time. A condition of his bond was that he was not to possess any firearms.

The task force began close surveillance of Tom Dillon in mid-October of 1992. The officers watched as Dillon made weekend jaunts of 75 to 125 miles around Belmont, Harrison, Tuscawarus, Holmes, Coshocton, and Carroll counties. Always by himself, Dillon drank beer and shot up traffic signs, electric meters, even cows and animals on his drives.

In November of 1992, detectives followed Dillon to a gun show in New Philadelphia where he purchased a .22 caliber rifle. The purchase was enough to arrest the suspect for violating the terms of the conditions set for bond in the silencer matter. The investigators faced an impossible decision. Although they now had enough to arrest Tom Dillon, they lacked corroborating evidence in the serial murders. Yet, with Ohio's deer season looming, they risked the chance he would kill again when an estimated 300,000 hunters descended on the state.

They decided against that chance.

Thomas Dillon was arrested for violating the conditions of his bond by purchasing a rifle on November 30, 1992. Authorities hoped a search of his residence, vehicles, and belongings would in some way tie him to the sportsmen's murders. They drew a blank.

Five days later another bond hearing was held regarding the illegal silencer charge. Desperate prosecutors revealed Dillon had become the prime suspect in five acts of what appeared to be random murder. The avalanche of publicity that followed the announcement turned out to be a key turning point in the case.

On December 4, 1992, a Stark County resident alerted the task force he had purchased a 6.5 x 55mm Swedish Mauser rifle from Tom Dillon at a Massillon gun show in the spring of 1992. The man turned the rifle, along with a receipt of purchase, over to detectives. Now able to place the rifle in Tom Dillon's possession at the time of the shootings, investigators matched bullets fired from the Mauser to those recovered from the bodies of Gary Bradley and Claude Hawkins. Dillon was indicted on two counts of aggravated murder, with death specifications, on January 22, 1993.

The media now took a serious look at the life of accused serial murderer Thomas Lee Dillon. Born in Canton, Ohio, on July 9, 1950, Dillon's father died of Hodgkin's disease when young Tom was only fifteen months old. Dillon told psychologists he viewed his mother as a cold, ambivalent person who neither praised nor chastised him. Classmates from Glenwood High School remembered him as a "loner" but little more. After high school, Tom attended Kent State University's Stark campus and later transferred to Ohio State, where he graduated in 1972. He immediately went to work as a draftsman for the Canton Water Department. In 1978, he married Catherine

Elsass, a nurse from Alliance, Ohio. In the mid-1980s Dillon found his way onto the local police radar when neighbors complained he was killing their dogs.

Dillon's shocked family and over a hundred onlookers packed the Noble County Courthouse on February 9, 1993, as Dillon was led to the proceedings, handcuffed and in leg shackles. Tom Dillon spent little time in pleading "not guilty" to murder charges in the wrongful deaths of Gary Bradley and Claude Hawkins. On May 22, 1993, a third murder charge followed for the homicide of Jamie Paxton. Three days later Dillon received the maximum three years and ten months in prison for his earlier federal firearms conviction. Before he could make his trial date, Dillon made calls from the jailhouse to WTOV-TV and the *Akron Beacon Journal* where he made a confessional rant. "I have major problems! I'm crazy! I want to kill! I want to kill!" he explained. The next day Dillon's lawyers proposed a plea bargain regarding the charges against their client.

On July 12, 1993, Thomas Lee Dillon stood before Judge John Nau in Noble County Common Pleas Court and blankly answered "guilty" as each charge against him was read. Observers noted no emotion in his voice. Noble County Prosecutor Lucian Young III called the plea agreement "the most practical solution." Dillon was sentenced on the spot to the maximum life in prison with no chance of parole for 165 years. Although Jean Paxton expressed relief the case was over, she noted Dillon's lack of remorse. "I think he's a pathetic coward," she said of Dillon. "He's taken the coward's way out of everything."

Later in July of 1993, convicted serial murderer Thomas Dillon came clean about other sick criminal acts he'd perpetrated against the people in eastern Ohio over the previous five years. He admitted setting fires and committing acts of vandalism in

Coshocton, Belmont, Guernsey, Carroll, Columbiana, and Tuscarawas counties, causing an estimated $2 million-plus in damage. Because of the plea deal, he was not tried for any of the offenses.

Tom Dillon, despite his protest, was sent to the Ohio maximum security facility in Lucasville. It's his current, and hopefully last, residence.

Fallen Angel

In 1987 a deputy for the Hamilton County Coroner's Office in Ohio's southwesternmost county began an autopsy of what he assumed was a death attributable to an unfortunate motorcycle accident. But when Dr. Lee Lehman performed the routine study of the victim's stomach, he noticed the distinct odor of "bitter almond," a sign of the presence of poisonous cyanide. Routine quickly gave way from a motor vehicle accident to a homicide investigation. The deceased had been a patient at Hamilton County's long-term health care facility, Drake Hospital, located in Cincinnati. Cincinnati police began an investigation.

The police started their investigation by requesting polygraph tests of all of the hospital personnel, visitors, or staff who may have had access to the victim. When it came time for thirty-five-year-old nursing assistant **Donald Harvey**'s turn on the lie-detecting device, he opted to forgo the test in lieu of confessing to the killing. Harvey was promptly arrested and charged with aggravated murder. He quickly pleaded not guilty by reason of insanity, declaring the death "an act of mercy." A trial date was set, and a Drake spokesperson declared the death a "singular incident." But other hospital staff feared otherwise.

ANGEL of DEATH
Donald Harvey

When Drake Hospital administration refused to listen to the suspicions of other employees who had noticed a an unusually high death rate around patients attended to by Donald Harvey, they took the story to Cincinnati's WCPO-TV newsman Pat Minarcin, who aired a thorough report of his stunning findings on June 23, 1987. Soon after, Harvey was in Hamilton County Common Pleas Court admitting guilt to twenty-eight separate killings. As part of a plea deal, he received multiple life terms in prison.

Amazingly, Harvey's story got worse when he admitted his murderous habits actually started sixteen years earlier when he was a nurse's aide at a medical facility in London, Kentucky. Harvey's victims weren't just hospital patients. He admitted poisoning other people to death, including the parents of his homosexual lover. Poisoning wasn't his only method either. He sometimes employed horribly painful tactics, including suffocation with plastic bags placed over his victim's head or rupture of a male victim's bladder via insertion of a coat hanger into the poor patient's catheter.

Despite guilty pleas to thirty-seven murders, a vile designation that makes him one of the most prolific serial killers in American history, Donald Harvey will never face the executioner because of plea agreements. He will likely spend the rest of his life at the Lebanon Correctional Institution in Warren County.

First Blood in Ohio

The media attention given to the case of serial killer/necrophiliac/cannibal/all-around sick psychopath **Jeffrey Dahmer** made the perverted degenerate a topic of conversation worldwide. What many don't know is Dahmer began his thirteen-year

DAHMER!
All-around sicko

killing spree shortly after his high school graduation in June 1978 while he was living with his father in the upscale Ohio area of Bath Township in western Summit County near Akron.

As Dahmer confessed years later, he picked up another teen, Steve Hicks, while Hicks was hitchhiking. Dahmer drove Hicks to his parents' place, where the two had sex and drank beer. When Hicks wanted to leave, Dahmer didn't like the idea and beat Steven over the head with a barbell, killing him.

In order to hide what he had done, Dahmer cut the body into pieces, packaged it up in plastic garbage bags, and buried the bags in the woods behind his house. His ugly habit had begun. That fall Dahmer enrolled at Ohio State University but flunked out after one semester with a GPA of only 0.45. He joined the army at the end of 1978 but was discharged after a couple of years for being an alcoholic. He returned to Bath for a time where, once back home, he dug up Hicks's body and pulverized the decomposing corpse with a sledgehammer, scattering the remains in the Bath Township woods afterwards.

Kirtland's Resident Terrorists

On August 19, 1984, **Jeffrey** and **Alice Lundgren** and their four children arrived at their new home in rural Kirtland in the northern part of Ohio. Jeffrey, a self-proclaimed "prophet of God," rented a run-down farmhouse and the family settled in. When an ensemble of young men and women proclaiming to be former members of the Reorganized Church of the Latter-day Saints joined the Lundgrens, neighbors assumed they were starting some sort of commune.

Choosing tiny Kirtland as their residence was no accident. The area is home to a historic temple built and maintained by the Mormon Church. Started in 1832 and dedicated in 1836, the Kirtland Temple was built when Latter-day Saints leader Joseph Smith, Jr., proclaimed he had received a revelation from God to construct the holy place in Kirtland.

But Jeffrey Lundgren, the "self-proclaimed prophet," had another view of the temple, that of the "promised land." Lundgren held a twisted doctrine that he was to lead his group in fulfilling an apocalyptic vision that would reclaim the Kirtland Temple. The task would require "blood sacrifice."

Lundgren ignored true Mormon beliefs and ruled his followers like a dictator. He led the men through paramilitary exercises in preparation for the violent takeover of the temple. The women were made to participate in bizarre sexual rituals. Nightly, Lundgren preached on the necessity for blood to be spilled in order for the group to see God in the flesh on earth. On April 17, 1989, a family within the group, the Averys (Dennis, Cheryl, and their three children), suffered the fruition of Jeffrey Lundgren's sick vision. The Averys were led one by one into a barn on the property where they were bound, blindfolded, and dumped into a pit. Jeff Lundgren then executed each with a .45 pistol.

Most of the cult was charged and found guilty for their participation in the Kirtland massacre. Jeffrey Lundgren was found guilty of, among other crimes, five counts of aggravated murder. He received the death penalty. On October 24, 2006, over seven years after the grisly murders, Lundgren may have had the opportunity to fulfill at least part of his heinous vision. He may have stood in judgment before God when he was executed by lethal injection at the Southern Ohio Correctional Facility in Lucasville.

BUCKEYE
STATE
MISCHIEVOUS
MISCELLANY

16

OHIO—THE HEART OF IT ALL! IT CERTAINLY IS!

We're a center for agriculture, football, and industry as well as a great place to live. We've also had our share of folks who, for one reason or another, have done some things that make us blush a little. To follow: a sampling of some unsavory Buckeyes who won't be riding in a hometown parade anytime soon.

XXX from Steubenville

Before she became porn queen **Traci Lords**, Nora Kuzma was born into this world in Steubenville, Ohio, on May 7, 1968. Lords opens her autobiography *Traci Lords: Underneath It All* by describing Steubenville as "a dirty little steel town" where she grew up on "the wrong side of the fence." One of four sisters in a blue-collar family, little Nora endured a violent, alcoholic father until her mother decided to move the girls out of harm's way. When the Kuzma girls and their mom moved in with the kids' great-grandmother, Nora found more violence and worry. The great-grandmother lived in a low-income housing development populated mostly by African-Americans. She suffered daily beatings at the hands of neighborhood children because of her race until her mother interceded. When Nora's father came to the housing project and violently beat her mother, the women of the family left Ohio in search of safety.

The road was not kind to the Kuzmas. When it came to making ends meet, jobs were scarce and money was soon gone so they returned to Steubenville, where Louis and Patricia Kuzma officially divorced. Things really didn't get better for Nora. She tells of being raped at age ten by a sixteen-year-old friend. Her mother met a new love interest while attending Ohio University. Things may have looked up when the boyfriend, Roger Hays, mother Patricia, and the four sisters made their way to Hollywood in search of a better life.

California didn't prove to be the right place for Roger Hays and Pat Kuzma, and they soon broke up. At age fifteen Nora had an abortion after becoming pregnant during a high school puppy love romance. Roger, the only adult Nora felt she could trust, helped arrange the abortion and used the opportunity to introduce fifteen-year-old Nora to the world of fake IDs and

TEEN PORN QUEEN!
Nora Kuzma (aka Traci Lords)

nude modeling. Barely a high school sophomore, Nora Kuzma was fifteen when *Penthouse* hired her for a photo shoot and suggested she choose a "sexy" stage name. Traci Lords was born: "Traci" a popular name Nora liked as a youngster, "Lords" in tribute to Jack Lord of the popular TV show *Hawaii Five-O* with an "s" added because Nora felt she was three people: herself, "Kristie," her fake ID name, and Traci, her new glamour name. As Lords put it: "I was high school sophomore Nora Kuzma by day and nude centerfold model Traci Lords by night."

Lords went on to become a famous porn star. Drug use and a strange lifestyle took their toll, however, and she found herself in trouble. When Traci turned eighteen, deeply entrenched in her decadent lifestyle, she claims she was kidnapped by the Federal Bureau of Investigation. In *Underneath It All*, Lords describes how she was awakened during an early-morning raid on her Los Angeles apartment, where she was handcuffed and whisked away to the downtown L.A. Federal Building to be told: "We know who you are, Nora." After going on to tell Lords she was part of a sting operation, they went on to reveal "they'd been gathering information for awhile." "You people knew the whole time?" Traci asked the feds. Realizing they'd been witness to her entire desperate career, she "went berserk."

"Hey," Lords says the detective told her, "what are you crying for? Tomorrow we're all going to be famous. Isn't that what you want?" Traci Lords has since found her way to "legitimate" acting. One thing's for sure, the little girl from Ohio had a tough road to the top.

Fleeing the Cornfields

One-time porno kingpin "Sultan of Smut" **John Holmes, aka Johnny Wadd**, also came out of Ohio's Pickaway

County. He was born John Curtis Estes in rural Ashville, Ohio, on August 8, 1944, to a religious fanatic, Mary. John was raised by Mary and an abusive, alcoholic stepfather named Harold. Holmes became a Bible student but, at the age of sixteen, found an exit out of Ohio by joining the U.S. Army.

By the time he was twenty, John moved to Los Angeles, where he worked as a driver until a female neighbor working in the porn industry suggested he try the business to make "good money." According to *Screw Magazine*, the legendary length of John's member was a whopping 12⅝ inches, making him a "natural" for porn flicks. His remarkable physical attribute garnered over two thousand appearances in adult movies that spanned over twenty years at an all-time-high pay rate of $3,000 a day. He even costarred with fellow Ohio native (and underage star at the time) Traci Lords.

In the late 1970s, the porn star became addicted to recreational drugs. By late 1979, he had lost all his XXX assets and entered a life of crime. By 1981 he was implicated in four murders, believed to be drug related, in the Laurel Canyon section of Los Angeles. The "King of Porn" was later acquitted of murder charges but served time in prison for related burglary and contempt-of-court charges.

Released in November 1982, Holmes returned to the porn business but found it far less lucrative than previous years. Still addicted to drugs, John was diagnosed with AIDS by 1985; he continued working in porn despite the disease until 1987. "Johnny Wadd" died of AIDS-related complications in a California VA hospital on March 13, 1988, at the age of forty-three. He once estimated he'd had sex with over 14,000 women on- and off-screen during his career.

*John Estes (aka John Holmes aka
Johnny Wadd) and friend*

Fun with Dick and Jane in Cleveland

Jane Fonda was deeply embroiled in her antiwar efforts in 1970 when she returned from a rally in Ontario, Canada, on November 2 by way of Cleveland's Hopkins International Airport. Upon her arrival in the States, customs officials discovered 105 vials of pills in Fonda's luggage. Assuming the activist actress was smuggling drugs into the country, they promptly took Ms. Fonda into custody and took her to an airport security office. There she allegedly assaulted a security officer while being detained. She was eventually booked into the Cuyahoga County Jail on charges of drug smuggling and assault. The arrest made front-page headlines around the country, which was deeply divided about the Vietnam War in general and Fonda's patriotic or treasonous activities, depending on your views, in particular.

When both charges were dropped, the story, if it was reported at all, seldom showed up before page six. But that wasn't the end of the story, according to Jane Fonda. In her 2005 autobiography *My Life So Far*, Fonda claims she was the target of a government operation organized to disrupt anti-war protesters' activities through a secret operation known as COINTELPRO.

Ms. Fonda describes COINTELPRO as a counter-intelligence program dreamed up by Federal Bureau of Investigation Director J. Edgar Hoover to "discredit members of the antiwar and militant black movements." She says COINTELPRO worked by "... infiltration, sabotage, intimidation, murder (directly assassinating or hiring rival groups to assassinate leaders), by framing activists for crimes the FBI committed, and through fake black propaganda—feeding journalists information

MOVIE STAR DRUG BUST!

Jane Fonda cuffed and jailed in Cleveland

139813
CLEVELAND
32 5 8 126
NOV 3 1970

through phony letters and inflammatory leaflets that slandered and discredited the targeted person."

Other than some negative publicity and fearful inconvenience on Jane Fonda's part, nothing came of the incident at the Cleveland airport. As for COINTELPRO's alleged efforts against the Hollywood star, Fonda concludes, "After extensive investigation of COINTELPRO, Senator Frank Church's Select Committee on Government Intelligence Activities pronounced it 'a sophisticated vigilante program aimed squarely at preventing the exercise of First Amendment rights of freedom and of association.' Seems the government felt it necessary to destroy democracy in order to save it. And look where it got us— Watergate and the first presidential resignation in U.S. history."

Dolly Takes on the Man

Speaking of rights granted by the Constitution of the United States, every rookie police officer and first-year law student studies the Fourth Amendment's implications as they relate to the landmark case of Mapp vs. Ohio. What many people don't know is the **Dolly Mapp** case came to the attention of the United States Supreme Court by way of the Cleveland Police Department. Search-and-seizure rules and rules of evidence changed forever in America from what started on the porch of Don "the Kid'" King in urban Cleveland during the early-morning hours of May 20, 1957.

On that day, at around three in the morning, two goons from the Cleveland mob exploded a bomb on the front porch of King's house at 3713 East 151st Street. Nobody was hurt but, needless to say, the occupants were shaken up. The police were not necessarily surprised by the attack, because they knew

King was a "clearinghouse" operator who ran a numbers game in downtown neighborhoods of Cleveland, collecting cash from runners who took wagers from local residents and paying the occasional winner. The Kid also dabbled in bookmaking and loan-sharking.

Cleveland vice cops knew King well, especially from a 1954 murder arrest for which the Kid had been acquitted after pleading self-defense. Most people in the Kid's line of work didn't talk to the police, so Cleveland officers were surprised when King broke the unwritten code of silence and went to the *Cleveland Plain Dealer* to finger a local mobster, Alex "Shondor" Birns, for the bombing.

Birns, a Jewish immigrant from Hungary, had done twenty-seven months in the penitentiary for income tax evasion starting in 1954. While Birns sat in jail, King and some others had horned in on the lucrative numbers game. The mobster didn't like it. In October 1956, Boss Birns sent emissaries to his rivals suggesting they each pony up $200 a week or pay the consequences.

Initially, the Kid and his pals agreed to pay, but by December the Kid decided the price was too high and dropped his payments to $100. By February King decided he didn't want to pay at all, cutting Shondor out of the action completely. Birns responded by literally "dropping the bomb." That's when Don King took the unprecedented step of naming the Hungarian and his henchmen in the press. One of the names he dropped was Virgil Ogletree, a Cleveland prizefighter who often spent time with his girlfriend, Dollree Mapp (better known as Dolly), in the Shaker Heights section of the city at 14705 Milverton Street. Looking for Ogletree, Cleveland Vice Squad Sgt. Carl Delau and two of his men headed to Dolly's on the afternoon of May 23, 1957. The officers found Dolly at home.

Dolly Mapp

Dolly Mapp had moved to Cleveland from her native Austin, Texas, as a baby. She was a tall and very attractive woman who had a penchant for dating prizefighters. She knew her way around the block when the vice squad knocked on her door that spring day, and she wasn't afraid to tell them so. Sgt.

Delau rang the buzzer to Mapp's second-floor apartment (she rented the first floor to tenants), and said, "Let me in, Dollree." Ms. Mapp looked out the upstairs window, but didn't say a word. Instead, she called her lawyer, Walter Greene, who advised her not to let the cops enter without a warrant.

Dolly called out the window for a warrant from Sgt. Delau, who said he had one even though he refused to produce it. The police were convinced Ogletree was inside, and they were determined not to let him slip through their fingers. Dolly was equally determined the cops weren't coming into her house until they produced a warrant. The stalemate lasted three hours until more police arrived on the scene. Lawyer Greene arrived about the same time.

At around 4:30 p.m., Greene stood protesting as the cops broke down Dolly Mapp's door. He protested more when they prevented him from going inside to witness the search. It had been a long day, and when the officers failed to find any sign of Virgil Ogletree on the premises, they decided to go on the proverbial "fishing expedition" to make the reticent Dolly Mapp pay for her stubbornness. Dolly continued to demand a search warrant, and Sgt. Delau continued to deny the request. When Mapp persisted, Delau produced a piece of paper but refused to let the protesting Dollree read it. At one point Mapp snatched the paper from the sergeant's hand and stuffed it down her blouse. Undaunted, Delau went after it.

The search eventually turned up Ogletree hiding in the first-floor apartment, but he proved of no use in the Don King case. Dolly Mapp seemed to be in the clear, but the inconvenienced police made a point of noting another find at the Mapp residence: "a quantity of books, pamphlets and photographs they described as 'obscene.'" They also found what they described as "betting slips," which they thought were used for gambling.

Dollree Mapp drew two charges that day: a misdemeanor

gambling charge for the betting slips and a felony charge for obscenity for the risqué books found in her basement. The gambling charge was quickly dismissed. The felony obscenity charge was a different matter. Judge Donald Lybarger of the Cuyahoga County Court ruled that the dirty books seized by Sgt. Delau were admissible in court regardless of the validity of any search warrant. Despite contradictory testimony between the police and the defendant, Mapp was convicted by a jury. By today's standards the material found in Dolly Mapp's house would seem tame, but in the 1950s pornography seemed to cause fear. Judge Lybarger sentenced Dollree Mapp to seven years in the Ohio Reformatory for Women.

Appeal seemed a natural course for Mapp's attorneys. The Ohio Supreme Court eventually ruled that the evidence seized was valid even if a search warrant was not. At a whopping cost of $8,000 1960 dollars, Dolly Mapp presented her case to the United States Supreme Court. The unresolved issues of unreasonable search and seizure were finally to be heard by the country's top legal authority. Oral arguments in the case of Mapp vs. Ohio were scheduled to be heard by the Supreme Court on March 29, 1961.

Eighty-two days later, the Supreme Court issued a ruling that has affected the American criminal justice system ever since. Justice Clark wrote for the majority: "Presently, a federal prosecutor may make no use of evidence illegally seized, but a state's attorney across the street may. Thus the state, by admitting evidence unlawfully seized, serves to encourage disobedience of the Federal Constitution which it is bound to uphold. ... Nothing can destroy a government more quickly than its failure to observe its own laws, or worse, its disregard of the charter of its own existence."

And so today we live with the sweeping results of the exclusionary rule: evidence seized in violation of the Constitution is not admissible in *any* criminal trial—federal or state. Ohio brought us to the place.

Billy Milligan + 23 = Not Guilty

On October 27, 1977, Columbus police detectives and a SWAT team served a search warrant at the apartment of twenty-two-year-old **Billy Milligan**. They arrested him for the rapes of three Ohio State University students. Milligan was charged with two separate incidents of early-morning abductions of women from the OSU Medical Center parking lot where he forced the victims to drive him to remote locations and raped them at gunpoint, then forced them to use credit cards or write checks to get money. Milligan's third victim was abducted in her car on Lane Avenue and forced to drive to the northwest part of Franklin County, where she too was raped and robbed.

Billy Milligan was a convicted felon who had done time at the state prison at Lebanon for robbery. University police were certain they had "the Ohio State Rapist." Two of the victims had positively identified Milligan as the rapist, and his finger-prints were lifted from the third victim's car. They were puzzled, then, on October 6, 1978, when Milligan pleaded not guilty by reason of insanity to three counts each of rape, kidnapping, and robbery. Even more bizarre was Milligan's contention that the Ohio State Rapist was actually a nineteen-year-old lesbian named Adelena. "Adelena," it was discovered, just happened to share a body with Billy Milligan.

Milligan was promptly sent to a psychiatric hospital in Athens, Ohio, for evaluation. There, doctors believed they discovered the existence of ten separate personalities existing within Billy Milligan. Author Daniel Keyes, in his book *The*

Minds of Billy Milligan, takes a detailed look at the history of what led to the identification of twenty-four of "the people inside." Keyes describes each personality, which often had physical traits very different from the "core" Billy, who was six feet tall and weighed 190 pounds. For example, Keyes describes "Ragen Vadascovinich," one of the more prominent personalities described by Milligan's psychiatrists, as:

> Age 23. The keeper of hate. His name is derived from "rage-again." Yugoslavian, he speaks English with a noticeable Slavic accent, and reads, writes, and speaks Serbo-Croatian. A weapons and munitions authority as well as a karate expert, he displays extraordinary strength, stemming from the ability to control his adrenaline flow. He is a communist and atheist. His charge is to protect the family. ...
> He dominates the consciousness in dangerous places. Weighs 210 pounds, has enormous arms, black hair and a long drooping moustache.

By December 4, 1978, an Ohio court was about to make a precedent ruling that's had far-reaching effects. At the Franklin County Courthouse, using psychiatric reports as the basis, Common Pleas Judge Jay C. Flowers used Section 2945.38 of the Ohio Revised Code to find Billy Milligan incompetent to stand trial. The idea of using the diagnosis of Multiple Personality Disorder (MPD) to determine a single suspect's criminal responsibility when an "alter" personality committed the crime was born out of the Milligan case and still exists today.

Authors Elyn R. Saks, a professor of law, psychiatry and behavioral sciences at the University of Southern California Law School, and Stephen H. Behnke, chief psychologist of the Massachusetts Mental Health Center and an instructor at Harvard, use the Milligan case in their book *Jekyll on Trial: Multiple Personality*

Disorder and Criminal Law. Once psychiatrists determined Milligan was not responsible for the rapes and robberies, and two of his "alter personalities," Adelena and Ragen, had committed the crimes, is it unfair to punish the singular Billy when there are other "innocents" inside? Saks and Benke say yes:

> The criminal responsibility of multiples seems straightforward if alter personalities are different people. The alter who committed the crime, if not meeting the legal definition of insanity, is responsible. The other alters, unless complicit in the act, are not. Because we cannot punish the guilty alter without punishing the other, innocent alters, we should find the multiple as a whole nonresponsible.

Billy Milligan's was the first, but certainly not the last, in the particulars of MPD that are argued in courtrooms and psychiatric communities to this day. As for Billy Milligan, Daniel Keyes answers the question, "What ever happened to Billy?" on his Web site www.danielkeyesauthor.com:

> After ten years of being transferred from one maximum security hospital to another (Lima, Dayton, Columbus, back to Athens, then Massillon and Columbus again), Billy Milligan was finally pronounced fused, "no longer suffering from a mental disorder," and was discharged from the Ohio mental health system and the Ohio courts, on August 1, 1991.

Keyes adds that he has written a second book, *The Milligan Wars*, covering what has happened to Milligan since his release. The book has yet to be published in the U.S.

Charlie Hustles ...

I'm guilty of one thing in this whole mess, and that's
I was a horseshit selector of friends.
—*Pete Rose, implying that acquaintances were
responsible for the bad press in the spring of 1999
during the inquiry on his betting on baseball.*

In February of 1989 rumors of **Pete Rose**'s betting on baseball
games surfaced in Baseball Commissioner Peter Ueberroth's office.
Rose, former star player and manager of the Cincinnati Reds, was
summoned to the commissioner's office, where he vehemently
denied the charges. By March of that year the allegations became
public, compelling Rose to tell the media, "I'd be willing to bet
you, if I were a betting man, that I never bet on baseball."

But attorney John Dowd, whom baseball hired to investigate
the allegations, had quite a different story to tell in his 225-page
report, which he turned in to Ueberroth's replacement in the commissioner's office, Bart Giamatti. Much of Dowd's report was
based on the testimony of a onetime close friend of Pete's named
Paul Janszen, who, like Rose, was a native of Cincinnati's west side.
Janszen was also a bodybuilder who acquired a small fortune by
trafficking in steroids and cocaine through a Cincinnati gym.
Janszen became a federal informant after authorities implicated
him in the drug ring. When the feds finished their job, Janszen
readily agreed to cooperate with Dowd in baseball's Rose investigation. Janszen made no secret of the fact he was angry at
Rose, who refused to pay back $30,000 he owed Janszen.

Commissioner Giamatti insisted the Dowd report was confidential, but when court officials released it to the media on
June 26, 1989, some startling items came to light. The report

charged that in 1985, 1986, and 1987, Rose had bet on numerous professional baseball games, including fifty-two Reds' games in '87 (all on the Reds to win), at a minimum of $10,000 a day. Despite Rose's denials that he bet on baseball, he reached an agreement with the commissioner's office by August of 1989 that banned him from baseball. Despite being declared "permanently ineligible," baseball's "Charlie Hustle" was given permission to apply for reinstatement after one year.

Effectively out of the game, at least for the time being, Pete found more trouble in April 1990 when he pleaded guilty to felony counts of making false tax returns by concealing income in 1985 and 1987. He was sentenced to a five-month term in the federal penitentiary at Marion, Illinois, where he drew an assignment to the prison machine shop. His sentence also included a thousand hours of community service and $50,000 in fines, and he was ordered to seek counseling for gambling addiction.

By September of 1997 Pete Rose made his first application for reinstatement into baseball. Commissioner Bud Selig all but ignored the request. Six years earlier, in 1991, the National Baseball Hall of Fame adopted a rule stating, "Any player on baseball's ineligible list shall not be an eligible candidate" for induction. Although fan support remained high for baseball's hit king, he was still denied reinstatement even after a November 2002 meeting with Selig where Rose finally fessed up to betting on baseball.

On January 5, 2004, Rose announced on ABC's *Good Morning America* that he did indeed bet on Major League Baseball games. He echoed the admission in his autobiography, *My Prison Without Bars*. There's still a street named after the famed slugger, Pete Rose Way, that runs through the southern section of downtown Cincinnati, and Pete's induction to the Hall of Fame remains a frequent topic for sports chat, but the odds of Pete Rose's reinstatement to Major League Baseball are anybody's bet.

HIT KING, GAMBLER, WOMANIZER
Pete Rose (left) with Cincinnati talk show host Bob Braun

Bibliography

If you'd like to read more about the subjects of this book, you may want to take a look at these books and articles used in research for **OHIO CONFIDENTIAL**.

Chapter 1

"American Justice." *Time*, January 2, 1928.

Holden, Craig. *The Jazz Bird*. New York: Simon & Schuster, 2002.

Stimson, George. *The Cincinnati Crime Book*. Cincinnati: Peasenhall, 1998.

Chapter 2

King, Jeffrey S. *The Rise and Fall of the Dillinger Gang*. Nashville: Cumberland House, 2006.

Chapter 3

King, Jeffrey S. *The Life and Death of Pretty Boy Floyd*. Kent, Oh.: Kent State University Press, 1999.

McMurty, Larry. *Pretty Boy Floyd*. New York: Simon & Schuster, 2002.

Chapter 4

Britton, Nan. *The President's Daughter.* New York: Elizabeth Ann Guild, 1927.

Dean, John. *Warren G. Harding.* New York: Times Books, 2004.

Hagood, Wesley. *Presidential Sex.* New York: Citadel Press, 1998.

Russell, Francis. *The Shadow of Blooming Grove: Warren G. Harding in His Times.* New York: McGraw-Hill, 1968.

Chapter 5

Badal, James Jessen. *In the Wake of the Butcher: Cleveland's Torso Murders.* Kent, Oh.: Kent State University Press, 2001.

Bardsley, Marilyn. "The Kingsbury Run Murders or Cleveland Torso Murders." Available at http://www.crimelibrary.com/serial _killers/unsolved/kingsbury/index_1.html.

Heimel, Paul. *Eliot Ness.* Nashville: Cumberland House Publishing, 2000.

Rasmussen, William T. *Corroborating Evidence: The Black Dahlia Murder,.* Santa Fe: Sunstone Press, 2005.

Taylor, Troy. "Dead Men Do Tell Tales: Torso Killer: History, Hauntings and the Mad Butcher of Kingsbury Run." Available at http://www.prairieghosts.com/torso.html.

Chapter 6

Fuller, M. Williams. *Axis Sally: The Most Listened-to Woman of WWII.* Santa Barbara, Calif.: Paradise West Publishing, 2004.

Kaelin, J.C., Jr. *Gerry's Front: Calling American Forces.* Audio CD of radio broadcast, available from http://www.earthstation1.com/ Merchant/merchant.mv?Screen=PROD&Store_Code=E&Product _Code=GFCAFAC&Category_Code=SB.

Chapter 7

Boertlein, John. "A Very Cold Case." *Cincinnati Magazine,* July 2006.

Chapter 8

Canfora, Alan. "US Government Conspiracy at Kent State—May 4, 1970." Available at http://www.alancanfora.com/?q=node/10.

Caputo, Philip. *13 Seconds: A Look Back at the Kent State Shootings.* New York: Penguin, 2005.

Dickson, Kenneth R. *Nothing Personal Just Business.* Self-published, 2006.

Kelner, Joseph and James Munves. *The Kent State Coverup.* Available from http://corppub.iuniverse.com/marketplace/backin-print/0595174922.html?id=7BmUTnGG.

Walsh, Denny. "The Governor and the Mobster." *Life,* May 2, 1999.

Chapter 9

Bugliosi, Vince. *Helter Skelter: The True Story of the Manson Murders.* New York: W.W. Norton, 2001.

Emmons, Nuel and Charles Manson. *Manson in His Own Words.* New York: Grove/Atlantic, 1988.

Udo, Tommy. *Charles Manson: Music, Mayhem, Murder.* London: Sanctuary, 2002.

Chapter 10

Ray, Elizabeth L. *The Washington Fringe Benefit.* New York: Dell, 1976.

Chapter 11

Flynt, Larry. *An Unseemly Man: My Life as Pornographer, Pundit and Social Outcast.* Chicago: IPG, 1997.

Chapter 12

Yonke, David. *Sin, Shame and Secrets: The Murder of a Nun, the Conviction of a Priest and Cover-up in the Catholic Church.* New York: Continuum, 2006.

Chapter 13

Cooper, Cynthia L. and Sam Reese Sheppard. *Mockery of Justice: The True Story of the Sam Sheppard Murder Case.* Memphis: Onyx, 1977.

Sheppard, Sam. *Endure and Conquer.* New York: World Publishing, 1966.

Pollack, Jack Harrison. *Dr. Sam: An American Tragedy.* New York: Avon, 1975.

Chapter 14

Anderson, Kevin. "Ulysses S. Grant's Lifelong Struggle With Alcohol." Available at http://www.historynet.com/historical_figures/3031671.html.

Balz, Dan. "Taft Admits Ethics Violations." *Washington Post,* August 19, 2005.

Boak, Josh. "Taft pleads no contest to state ethics charges." *Toledo Blade,* August 18, 2005.

Cutler, Jessica. *The Washingtonienne: A Novel.* New York: Hyperion, 2005.

Grant, Ulysses S. *Personal Memoirs of U.S. Grant.* New York: Modern Library, 1999.

Latiak, Ted. "Ohio Judge in Courthouse Sex Scandal." Available at http://www.cnn.com/2005/LAW/10/20/judge.sex/index.html.

Martin, Joel and William J. Birnes. *The Haunting of the Presidents: A Paranormal History of the U.S. Presidency.* New York: New American Library, 2003.

Chapter 15

"Confession from a Killer Doc." CBS News, October 18, 2000.

Dahmer, Lionel. *A Father's Story.* New York: William Morrow, 1998.

Davis, Donald A. *The Jeffrey Dahmer Story: An American Nightmare.* New York: St. Martin's, 1991.

Lohr, David. "Arsenic Anna: The True Story of Anna Marie Hahn." Available at http://www.crimelibrary.com/notorious_murders/women/anna_hahn/index.html.

———. "The .22 Caliber Killings." Available at http://www.crimelibrary.com/serial_killers/partners/lewingdon_bros/1.html.

———. "Hunter of Humans: The True Story of Thomas Lee Dillon." Available at http://www.crimelibrary.com/serial_killers/predators/dillon/1.html

Knox David, Jolene Limbacher and Kim McMahan. "Hunter of Humans: Man Who'd Aim at Anything Is Finally the Law's Target." *Akron Beacon Journal,* January 24, 1993.

Newton, Michael. *Hunting Humans: An Encyclopedia of Modern Serial Killers.* Port Townsend, Wash.: Loompanics, 1990.

Stewart, James B. *Blind Eye: How the Medical Establishment Let a Doctor Get Away with Murder.* New York: Simon & Schuster, 1999.

Stimson, George. *The Cincinnati Crime Book.* Cincinnati: Peasenhall, 1998.

Whalen, William and Bruce Martin. *Defending Donald Harvey: The Case of America's Most Notorious Angel-of-Death Serial Killer.* Cincinnati: Emmis, 2005.

Stalter-Sassé, Cynthia and Peggy Murphy-Widder. *The Kirtland Massacre: The True and Terrible Story of the Mormon Cult Murders.* New York: Zebra, 1992.

Chapter 16

Fonda, Jane. *My Life So Far.* New York: Random House, 2005.

Keyes, Daniel. *The Minds of Billy Milligan.* New York: Bantam, 1994.

Lords, Traci. *Traci Lords: Underneath It All.* New York: HarperCollins, 2003.

Persico, Deborah A. *Mapp v. Ohio: Evidence and Search Warrants.* Landmark Supreme Court Cases. Berkeley Heights, N.J.: Enslow, 1997.

Saks, Elyn R. and Stephen H. Behnke. *Jekyll on Trial: Multiple Personality Disorder and the Criminal Law.* New York: New York University Press, 1997.

Sokolove, Michael E. *Hustle: The Myth, Life and Lies of Pete Rose.* New York: Simon & Schuster, 1990.

Index

Page numbers in italics indicate photographs.

About the *AUTHOR*

John Boertlein knows the mean streets. He's seen more than his share of sex, scandal, murder, and mayhem. He was a police officer for nearly thirty years, achieving the rank of police sergeant in the Cincinnati Police Department, where he served from 1981 to 2006. He also served in the Covington (Kentucky) Police Department from 1978 to 1981. He holds a license to teach for the Ohio Peace Officer's Training Association and was an instructor at the Cincinnati Police Academy. He is the author of *Howdunit: How Crimes Are Committed and Solved* (Writer's Digest Books, 2002) and *Today in History: Elvis* (Emmis Books, 2006) and is a frequent contributor to *Cincinnati Magazine*.